I0503572

HOMEOWNERS
INSURANCE GUIDE

Florida 2018/19
MARTYN G. D. BELBEN

HOMEOWNERS INSURANCE
CLAIMS HANDLING PRACTICES

HOT ISSUES
ASSIGNMENT OF BENEFITS
OPTION TO REPAIR

Visit Our Website

www.flhoguide.com

ISBN-13 9781717430786
ISBN-10 1717430783

BISAC - Business and Economics / General

Published by
Homeowners Insurance Research, Inc.
P. O. Box 4647
Fort Lauderdale, Florida 33338, U.S.A.
877 772 4006 - 954 772 4006
Fax. 954 772 1931
mbelben@flhoguide.com

PROLOGUE

Every effort has been made to ensure that the information contained in this guide is accurate and may be relied upon as such by the reader.

Statistics contained in the insurance carrier section in Chapter 30 at the end of this guide, were provided by the Florida Department of Financial Services, Department of Insurance and other reliable research web sites and therefore, are expected to be correct.

The comments made in this guide relating to unethical and generally serious misconduct by those engaged in the claims business, on the carrier side of the equation, are based upon facts, extracted from analysis of actual claim files over a period of years preceding the dates of research.

At various times over the past twenty five years, plaintiffs' attorneys and others have attempted to curb the carriers escalating unfair, and illegal, claims handling practices using language that has taken "the high road."

Those efforts have fallen on deaf ears, and the carriers' lust for greater and greater profits, and surpluses, has now evolved into nothing short of a machine that openly defrauds its policyholder customers, in the manner of a thinly disguised, variation of a Ponzi scheme.

Moreover, the Florida Department of Insurance, whose portfolio includes protecting Florida policyholders from predatory insurance companies' unfair, illegal, and perhaps criminal conduct in the handling of claims, and a succession of individuals sitting in lofty chairs, acting in the role of Insurance Commissioner, have taken no action whatsoever to curb this illegal activity.

Since the introduction to the marketplace of the McKinsey claims handling doctrine of "Deny, Delay and Defend" twenty five years ago, as far as I have been able to ascertain, there has been only one case of a Florida insurance company being censured and fined for it's illegal practices in the handling of homeowners' claims; but not a single insurance company official, or an adjuster representing the carrier, at any level, has been disciplined for his role in the illegal handling of policyholders' claims.

The McKinsey doctrine of handling claims involves, I say again, unethical, illegal, and some would say criminally fraudulent claims handling practices.

It is high time to expose this conspiratorial condition of corrupt failure to act, and virtual complicity by these inactions by the Department, and the Florida Legislature, which are construed as tacit approval and encouragement to the insurance carriers of their claims handling practices.

Throughout this guide, I have used the pronouns, "he" and "his" in a general context when I should have used "he/she/they."

To have done that would have been unnecessarily cumbersome. Please, therefore, excuse my license with the language.

LEGAL ISSUES

Where it seems to me to be appropriate, throughout this guide I have made comments, statements, and used language which may be considered to have a legal flavor.

However, nothing written in this guide is intended to be, nor should any such language be interpreted to be legal opinion or legal advice.

The language used in this guide reflects my own personal thoughts and opinions, as an educated legal layman, and are based upon targeted professional education, knowledge and experience gained over a period of over sixty-four years in the property, casualty, contractor's "All Risks" / builder's risk, major civil engineering and marine claims losses, handling routine, major, and "mega" claims in over seventy countries, round the globe.

In some, if not most of those jurisdictions, qualified loss adjusters, on a daily, routine basis, investigate, adjust (including making legal arguments, making legal decisions and negotiating claims and settlements with attorneys), and generally "handle" to a conclusion a myriad of claims, with mostly authority to bind underwriters to both policy liability and the quantum of loss.

Moreover, in the United Kingdom, and in former British colonial jurisdictions, it is standard practice for the loss adjuster handling a claim file which is in suit, to supervise the strategy and tactics used by attorneys, on behalf of the carrier, be they either a solicitor or a barrister, so that they work together on a file; and the formal "instructions" are conveyed by the loss adjuster to the legal professionals. In those jurisdictions, attorneys are "instructed" by the loss adjuster, standing in the shoes of the insurer.

Conversely, in the United States, it appears that attorneys are given a free hand to handle a claim file or suit, if the claim is in suit, as they please without consultation with the client, or the client's representative.

In the United States, loss adjusters are prohibited from handling many of those claims and if they were to do so, they would be charged with "practicing law without a license."

Each system has its own pros and cons.

Inevitably, legal language has found a way into my vocabulary when handling claims.

However, I am not a lawyer, and since being based in the United States, I have been at pains not to cross the line into the practice of law.

If I use language which an attorney might find borderline, I mean them no disrespect, and it is completely unintentional.

When, not if - but when a reader finds it necessary to seek advice from an attorney, and your situation involves a first party property claim, I believe it would be in your best interests to visit the website of the Florida Association of Public Insurance Adjusters (www.fapia.net) where you will find a plethora of top drawer lawyers advertising their services, experienced as practitioners at the Florida Property Plaintiffs' Bar.

All of them will give you advice upon which you may rely, and most of them will offer you a "Florida Bar" contingency contract.

But, a word of caution: because your cousin's brother-in-law is a practicing attorney, does not mean that he knows anything about Florida, property insurance law.

The wrong choice might cost you dearly.

Choose your professional advisor wisely.

INDEX

INDEX

CHAPTER 1

TRADITIONAL CLAIMS HANDLING

The global insurance industry has changed dramatically over the last twenty five (25) years, but only a relatively very small proportion of Florida homeowners has noticed the difference.

Why? Because relatively few Florida homeowners have suffered a loss and have filed a claim with their insurance companies.

Those Florida policyholders who have suffered a loss and have filed a claim with their insurance companies probably have good reason to remember the experience.

Twenty five years ago, when a homeowner filed a claim, the circumstances of loss and the merits and quantum of the loss were investigated by a trained, knowledgeable, experienced and licensed loss adjuster representing the insurance company.

The investigation included determining when, where, why and how a loss occurred; whether the loss was covered by an insured "proximate cause" of loss, or an "insured peril" and, if so, the extent of the damage to the property, (including all the hidden damage); and the cost of restoring that damaged property to its pre-loss condition.

The field adjuster's estimate of the cost of restoring the damaged property to its pre-loss condition was based upon the then current contractors' prices for the location of the loss.

In addition, the field adjuster included in his estimate all the "add-on" items that he was required to include by law, whether those laws were created by statutes passed by the Florida legislature, or created by Florida Case Law, which are laws created by Florida Courts during actual trials and/or rulings by the Court (Judges).

Finally, the field adjuster would adjust the loss in accordance with the terms, conditions, limitations and deductibles of the policy, if any, issued to the policyholder, and applicable laws, and make recommendations to his management with respect to settlement.

Final settlement checks were then sent to the insured policyholder, usually within a time period of two to four weeks from the date of the loss, depending upon the amount of paperwork required by management and the insurance company's reinsurers.

Both the insurance carrier and their customer policyholder were satisfied.

The insurer had made good on its promises in its policy, they had treated their customer policyholder fairly and reasonably, and they had made a prompt settlement.

This system had stood the test of time for over four hundred years.

Also, by a silent but understood philosophy, or commonly understood practice, the property insurance industry as a whole had become a quasi-service industry which managed to combine, on the one hand, the principle that they were providing a vital service to the insured homeowner/customer, while on the other hand, running their businesses with utmost integrity, fairness and good faith, and the absolute trust each had in the other (the insurance company and the policyholder), and a reasonable and acceptable profit was made.

The result was that the insurance industry, globally, and over time, came to enjoy the envy and the unimpeachable respect of every other business community, in every conceivable profession, endeavor, venture and calling, worldwide.

After four hundred years of creating this gigantic, unbelievably successful, worldwide industry, the whole system changed, almost overnight, and crashed in 1992.

CHAPTER 2

THE NEW CONCEPT OF CLAIMS HANDLING

In September, 1992, the then President & CEO of Allstate Insurance hired McKinsey & Co., a New York firm of business management consultants, to investigate Allstate's business, and make recommendations for changes to improve their profits, or their "bottom line."

The essence of the McKinsey doctrine is using unfair, and illegal claims handling practices which have become known as **DENY, DELAY AND DEFEND.**

Most states, including Florida, have made the entire McKinsey doctrine of claims handling practices illegal and actionable.

However, **DENY, DELAY AND DEFEND** are the tools now used by insurers to increase their profits, beyond their wildest dreams, by denying, delaying and defending licit and valid claims without a legitimate reason.

What could be better for unscrupulous men. They simply could not believe their good fortune.

Forty years ago, perhaps more, but long before McKinsey & Co. became a player in the insurance industry, the President and CEO of one of the world's largest insurance conglomerates, based in the United States, was interviewed by a reporter of a large, high circulation, international business magazine.

He was asked by the interviewer, "Why did you choose the insurance industry for your career, a career in which you have been singularly and enormously successful, and from which you have earned a very considerable, personal fortune?"

The interviewee replied, I paraphrase: "Are you kidding? It is the only industry in the Universe where you get paid up front for something that may never happen; and if it does happen, you can delay the hell out of both the claims process, and the claim's progress through the system, which is easily manipulated, and make a lot of money hanging on to our customers' money for as long as we can. When you do have to pay, you evade paying as much of their claim, or demand as we can."

McKinsey took it to a new level.

McKinsey's theory is that every business of any size should be divided into separate departments, with each department having its own set of accounts, and its profit target.

McKinsey soon realized that there was a major stumbling block in using their usual template for an insurance company, which they would have to overcome.

The stumbling block was this: The claims department of an insurance company has no revenue.

The cost of operating a claims department has always been a net loss situation, and the challenge to every claims manager had always been to keep operating expenses and outgoing payments on claims reasonably low, without ruining the company's reputation for fair, competent and equitable claims handling practices.

McKinsey's plan was to change the way that Allstate did business and convince its Board of Directors that their attitude to their handling claims was out dated, and needed to change to a totally different mindset.

Allstate's directors made a choice. They climbed aboard the McKinsey bandwagon with unabashed glee.

McKinsey's system for the insurance market generates a "virtual income" (to use a modern term) by denying a valid claim, often without any investigation; misrepresenting the policy coverage to the policyholder by misapplying exclusions in the policy coverage, and/or taking the exclusion out of context to make an illicit argument leading to a denial of coverage.

In the majority of claims, where a denial of coverage is clearly unsustainable, the tactic is to under "scope" the loss (the scope is a line-by-line list of everything that has to be done to restore the damaged property to its pe-loss condition), to fraudulent extremes, including ignoring the factors and procedures which are required by Florida statute law and/or case law, thus enabling, by use of their estimating computer software, to short change an offer of settlement to the policyholder, usually reducing the final settlement offer by as much as 75% or even 80% and sometimes as much as 90%, so that the policyholder only receives 10% of the amount he is actually entitled to recover.

The "savings" on payments made that is achieved is a "virtual income." No records are kept of these savings, but they are reflected in actual, and dramatic improvements to the "bottom line."

If there is no public adjuster involved it is difficult for the policyholder to understand what is going on, and how he is being short changed.

If the policyholder accepts the offer of settlement and signs a policyholder's release. settlement is rapid and the desk adjuster, who handles the paperwork, receives a merit bonus.

When a policyholder has a loss and files a claim, instead of being treated with courtesy and professionalism, they are now treated as if they were criminals attempting to defraud the insurance company.

In fact, the exact opposite is true.

Yes. The boot is on the other foot, on every claim, without exception. The deliberate intent to defraud the policyholder as practiced by the insurance companies, is rampant and very successful.

This conduct is monstrous and unethical, and violates the Code of Ethics to which every insurance professional, licensed by the state of Florida, including those insurance executives who are not required to be licensed, but with which they are nevertheless required by law to comply. Yet, today, insurance companies corporate operating policies totally ignore their statutory duty to comply with the Code of Ethics (which supposedly is monitored by the Florida Department of Insurance), with total impunity from any disciplinary action by the Department.

In the twenty-five years that the insurance industry has used the McKinsey doctrine of claims handling practices, there has been only one instance of disciplinary action taken against an insurance company, a fine imposed by the Florida Department of Insurance, against **Universal Property & Casualty Insurance Company, of Fort Lauderdale, Florida which was fined $1.26 million for unfair claims handling practices in May, 2013. Reportedly, this fine was reduced, by** negotiation, from a very much larger figure. **One might well ask: Why? Don't ask! You know why!!**

But, not a single employee of any insurance company, either at executive level or otherwise, has been disciplined for the constant, day-by-day, every day, flagrant, illegal and fraudulent claims handling practices.

Not a single person has been fined; not a single person has had his license to conduct insurance business been revoked; not a single person has been disciplined in any way.

This unspeakably corrupt inaction by the Florida Department of Insurance, and the Florida Legislature, speaks volumes, not the least of which is their tacit approval of the insurance companies' methods of handling homeowners' claims and, by turning a blind eye, approves and encourages the insurance companies fraudulent and criminal conduct.

If a licensed (and bonded) public adjuster failed to comply with a minor statute with which he is obliged to comply, his license would be revoked in a heartbeat.

It's those bulging, little brown envelopes doing their thing again, and again, and again, ad infinitum!

Florida's laws don't mean anything to the insurance industry. Those laws are ignored with studious impunity; their fraudulent conduct is ignored by Florida

Legislators, and those "do-nothing" geniuses who are just "there" to collect everyone knows what, session after session, year after year.

It's those bulging, little brown envelopes, which carry and spread so much influence.

Under DENY, DELAY AND DEFEND, when a policyholder makes a claim under his policy today, the insurance company sends out a field adjuster to the insured property to inspect the damage, write the scope of loss, and determine whether there is an exclusion in the policy which they can use to their advantage. If that scenario is a non-starter a low-balled offer of settlement is made usually about 20% of what the insured homeowner is entitled to recover by his policy.

In reality, this is just going through the motions.

The field adjuster, whether he be a company employee, or an "independent" adjuster, hired directly by the insurance company or by an "independent" firm of adjusters, has no authority to discuss policy coverage with the policyholder, or the public adjuster if one has been retained.

These estimators, and that is all they are, are trained to record in their scope of loss only the damage that is visible. If they cannot see damage, then damage does not exist.

In the event, inevitably, the company's estimate is most often flawed and worthless. Yes. It gives the company some figures to work with, to set a Reserve against the loss, for statistical purposes.

In addition, the field adjuster is no longer obligated to provide the policyholder with a copy of his estimate, which used to be required by law. But that requirement was repealed by the Florida legislature to make it easier for the insurance companies to short change and defraud their customers.

It's those bulging, little brown envelopes doing their work again!

The field adjuster's estimate is reviewed by the supervising desk adjuster, whose job it is to remove from the estimate any item which the company management deems to be an "inflation of the estimate," which includes deleting from the estimate all the "add-on" items which are required to be included in the estimate by Florida statute law. Particular attention is paid to these add-on items, which a public adjuster will have included in his estimate, (a copy of which is always provided to a policyholder), with a copy also to the insurance company's field adjuster.

For example: If the ceiling and/or walls of a room have suffered damage by a roof leak during a violent windstorm or rainstorm, the insurance company's field adjuster's estimate will show, "paint part of the ceiling and part of the walls, one coat." Items which are statutorily required to be included in the carrier's estimate are nowhere to be found.

By contrast, a public adjuster's estimate will provide for replacement of the damaged ceiling drywall, insulation, sealing and prepping the damaged areas; and then "paint the walls and ceiling, as original, two coats." In addition, by statute, the public adjuster's estimate will include (if any) prepping and painting of baseboards, quarter round, door(s) and trim; and window frames, two coats as is contractors' standard practice of paint application.

None of the add-on items listed in the Public Adjuster's estimate are ever agreed by the insurance company, until they have no choice, notwithstanding the fact that these items are required to be included, by Florida statute law, which is reprinted verbatim, later in this guide, and which is often referred to as "The Matching Statute." The insurance companies characterize these add-on items as "inflating an estimate," because public adjusters are paid a percentage of the amount paid by the insurance company.

No. The reason these items are included in the estimate is that Florida statutes require every claim to be adjusted **"in accordance with the terms and conditions of the policy, and the laws of this state."**

The applicable statutes could not be clearer, yet all, **repeat, all the insurance companies ignore these statutes**, to one degree or another.

Having made a low-balled offer of settlement to the insured policyholder, and having had that offer rejected by the policyholder, the company then embarks upon the second phase of **DENY, DELAY AND DEFEND**, by invoking its delaying tactics.

The insurance company will first hire a firm of defense attorneys with instructions to demand that the policyholder sit for an Examination Under Oath (EUO).

An EUO is a tool inserted in the policy as a **CONDITION** which means that the policyholder **must** obey the demand, and failure to comply with that demand renders the claim voidable at the insurer's option. More on a **"Condition"** in the policy later in this guide.

An appointment is scheduled for the policyholder to sit for the examination under oath some three, four or six months into the future. As the date for this EUO draws near, defense counsel for the insurance company, cancels and reschedules the examination, again three, four or six months further into the future. This tactic is repeated three or four times to prolong the "delay" in handing the claim. Very soon, the period of delay becomes extended, and might run into a total of six or even eight years or longer, depending upon the amount of the policyholder's claim.

The policyholder, having received and rejected a low-balled offer of settlement, has two cards up his sleeve, one or both of which he may now play.

Card 1. Since the delay period has been invoked, by the insurance company, the policyholder may demand by Florida statute, payment of the amount offered by the insurance company (to settle) as "undisputed funds."

Undisputed funds may be demanded at any time after 90 days from the date of loss, and the policyholder may bank and use those funds without prejudicing his right to continue prosecuting the insurer for his full recovery, known as a "full indemnity" for his loss.

Card 2. The policyholder has a second card he may now play, preferably after he has received the insurance company's check for the "undisputed funds."

The card presents itself as a "Demand for Appraisal" of the amount of his loss. However, the policyholder should be careful in playing this card because, although the appraisal process is binding on both the insurer and the policyholder, there are now some potentially negative factors inherent in the appraisal process, which are a recent development.

The insurance company appoints its appraiser, and pays its appraiser's fees, usually of the order of $750.00 to $1,250.00 depending upon the complexity of the loss.

The policyholder appoints his appraiser, and pays his appraiser's fees, again usually $750.00 to $1,250.00.

The two appraisers then, by mutual agreement, pick an Umpire, who decides any issues upon which the two appraisers, down the road, cannot agree.

The two appraisers then meet on site at the insured dwelling and they each write their own estimate, and try to settle their disagreements, if any, as between each other. If they are successful in reaching an agreement, the appraisal process is completed by each appraiser signing an Appraisal Award. Such an award is binding on the insurance company and the policyholder.

If the two appraisers cannot agree, they take those disputed issues to the Umpire, who hears both sides of the argument from the appraisers, and makes a decision on each issue submitted for his consideration.

Two signatures by any two of the three parties to the appraisal process sets the amount of the loss, which is then binding on both the insurance company and the policyholder, but subject to the terms, conditions, limitations and deductible(s) of the insurance policy.

The two principals in the appraisal process, the insurance company and the policyholder, each pay 50% of the Umpire's fee.

This sounds well and good, but there can be snags.

By the terms of the Appraisal process, until relatively recently, neither the insurance company nor the policyholder could have had any input whatsoever with either the selection of the Umpire or the Umpire's involvement in the appraisal process.

The reason for this was to ensure, as much as possible, that the appraisal process was totally independent of the two principals, the insurance company and the policyholder.

However, in recent years, insurance companies have been starting to influence their appointed appraisers in the selection process of the Umpire.

State Farm, for example, provide their chosen appraiser with a list of "acceptable potential umpires," from which list their appraiser is expected to make a choice for submission to his opposite number, the appraiser for the policyholder. Why, because those individuals on State Farm's list of acceptable umpires, as is well known in the industry, will do the insurance company's bidding. Essentially, as a generality, they will do as they are told to do by State Farm.

Other insurance companies do the same thing, and the appraisal "waters" have become tainted by potentially corrupt interference in the appraisal process by the insurance companies. Today, to invoke the Appraisal Clause in the policy and demand appraisal of a loss is more of a crap shoot, than it used to be say five years ago.

Today, some Umpires feel so intimidated by the insurance companies that they fear being "struck off" the lists of acceptable umpires because they have been deemed to be too generous in their awards to policyholders, and thereby risking the loss of a proportion of their income as professional insurance property claims Umpires.

In reality, they truly have a fine line to walk.

The answer to this dilemma, is obvious:

1. The Circuit Court having jurisdiction in the particular area of the location of the insured dwelling at issue should maintain a list of all qualified and available

Umpires practicing in the Circuit's area by, say zip code. Each Judge in that Circuit shall have a rotation for, say one week, to appoint the next Umpire from the list, in rotation, without any input whatsoever from either the insurance company or the policyholder.

2.   If any judge discloses a conflict of interest in any particular matter, a stand-by, alternative secondary judge, possibly the next judge in rotation, should make the selection of the umpire, again without any input from either side.

The rotation would continue, week by week.

Such a system would prevent the intervention of the insurance carrier into the appraisal equasion.

Just a suggestion. And, it's not rocket science.

If the policyholder elects not to go the Appraisal route, but continues to try to withstand the delaying tactics of the insurance company by staying the course, there are other tactics employed by the insurance companies to wear down the most determined policyholder.

We are assuming by now, that the policyholder has hired an attorney, who is winding his way through the court system.

We just touched on the first phase of the delaying process, by demanding that the policyholder sit for an examination under oath.

The next stage, and we are now probably two or three years into the adjustment of a relatively simple loss, usually, is for the insurance company to instruct their attorney to close his file. The insurance company then appoints another firm of attorneys to re-start the whole delaying process again, from the beginning.

Then, the policyholder receives yet another demand, from the new attorneys, to sit for another Examination Under Oath, again scheduled three, four or six months into the future and the whole game of musical chairs starts all over again.

This practice of DENY, DELAY AND DEFEND is an abomination to most career insurance professionals, of the old, pre-McKinsey school.

Another way to characterize this conduct is to say that these tactics are used as tools, to wear the claimant down to the point where they either walk away from their claim, or dig in their heels and be as determined as the insurance company in pursuing their claim, as they are in trying to get them to walk away.

These are just strategies and tactics being used to eventually fleece you out of your rightful entitlement under the terms and conditions of your policy, which is called your "proper indemnity," and persuade you to settle at very much less than you actually deserve.

Of course, these shameful and illegal tactics cost the insurance company vast amounts of money in attorneys' fees and costs, which they habitually blame upon "public insurance adjusters," "unscrupulous contractors" and "shady attorneys." Look who's talking!

Insurance company regulators in Florida have taken no action whatsoever to curb the use of any or all of these unfair, illegal and fraudulent claims handling practices and tactics, which have been deemed "officially" to be "Unfair Claims Handling Practices" by Florida statutes, but with weak and insufficient remedies at the "breach of contract" level. Perhaps, the imposition of a multiplier of ten (X10) added to an indemnity award by a court as "liquidated damages" over and above the contractual damages for breach of contract, might serve to curb these illegal practices, somewhat.

Attorneys will tell you, fraud is very difficult to prove. Maybe. But nothing worth doing is ever easy.

That is the challenge. They are right, it's not easy, but it's not rocket science either. Enough is Enough!

It is way past time for the McKinsey doctrine, and the plague of **DENY, DELAY AND DEFEND** to be run out of town.

The movement has to start somewhere.

CHAPTER 3

THE PLAGUE IN PRACTICE

The McKinsey doctrine of **DENY, DELAY AND DEFEND** quickly became an exceptionally successful strategy for handling claims, and the system paid off for the insurance companies, in spades. How was this achieved? By radically changing the way they do business which included, but was not limited to denying legitimate claims arbitrarily, and becoming hostile if the policyholder(s) refused to accept their denials of coverage, using unfair, illegal and mostly fraudulent tactics to delay a denied but legitimate claim for months, and perhaps years, and then offering a settlement dramatically short changing the policyholder.

The reality was, and is, that the insurance companies charge high premiums, and seek premium increases almost annually, while short changing and defrauding their policyholder(s) out of proper and equitable indemnity settlements.

This system, it bears repeating, is nothing more than a variation of a PONZI scheme, without any accountability to industry regulators, or any fear of retribution whatsoever.

For whatever reasons, successive Insurance Commissioners have given every insurance company, including, Citizens Property Insurance Corporation, a free ride to conduct their businesses as an insurance scam of the worst kind, which victimizes policyholders who have suffered a loss, when they are most vulnerable to being cheated, scammed and defrauded, out of their rightful and proper indemnity recovery.

Sometimes, policyholder(s) are so traumatized by this conduct that they just walk away from their claims, just to be free of the hostility, and the fraudulent conduct of the insurance company, because they feel powerless to obtain any reasonable relief.

They need to be free of the stink of their insurance company and breathe some fresh air.

Deny, Delay and Defend has now become the "normal expectation in claims handling practices" by all insurance companies. Fraud, by any other name, is still fraud.

Today, the only consideration is the insurance companies call for greater, and greater profits.

There is no consideration or compassion given to policyholders who suffer a loss and have to file a claim for which indemnity they have paid a high premium. The industry is no longer a quasi-service industry but is now an enterprise whose individual players are criminal co-conspirators trading as an insurance company. They don't care what their policies promise. Every claim is only about the money, and how much the insurer can avoid - no, evade from paying the policyholder, using whatever means they choose to use. If those means are fraudulent and/or criminal, so what, they don't care because no-one else cares, and they are fire proof. They have absolutely no fear of any consequences whatever, because they have a free ride, guaranteed.

Not even Florida government officials, whose job it is to regulate, oversee and enforce insurance laws when insurance companies cross the line between legal, and illegal, and/or criminal conduct, take any notice.

Notwithstanding this change in the way claims are handled, insurance company executives will tell anyone who will listen that things are just the same as they always were. They emphasize that they have the same infrastructure, the same concern for their policyholders (SIC), the same insurance policies, but with more exclusions and/or limitations than ever, most particularly in those areas of insured property that are most susceptible to Florida windstorms (which is why policyholders buy coverage!), and the kicker - "Yes. Claims will still be paid."

YES, claims will still be paid, but only if policyholders are willing to accept a minuscule percentage of the amount they are actually entitled to recover under their policy.

Adjusters representing insurance companies, whether they be staff adjusters or "independent" adjusters no longer have any authority to "adjust" claims, per se.

Their only duty is to write a scope of loss which lists the work necessary to repair some of the damage, ignoring all the hidden damage, because to pay for damage that cannot be seen, because it is behind walls or ceilings, reduces profits. However, Florida statutes prescribe that **all damage, including hidden damage**, be included in the scope of loss and the subsequent estimate that is generated from that scope.

In the twenty five years that the McKinsey doctrine has been used in the handling of claims, there has not been a single disciplinary action taken against any insurance company staff or field adjuster, or desk adjuster; or any independent adjuster employed by an insurance company, who has deliberately and intentionally written a low balled estimate in violation of Florida statutes.

Not a single one.

Yet, thousands of low balled and fraudulent estimates are written every day, and many of them become public records in law suits for breach of contract.

But, fraud is difficult to prove, or so we are told.

Moreover, one, and only one instance of disciplinary action has been taken by the Florida Department of Insurance against an insurance company, either by way of sanctions or other action, for insurance company employees habitually and as a frequent, daily practice of requiring or causing a low balled estimate to be written, in violation of Florida statutes relating to fair claims handling practices,

Successive Florida Government officials employed at the Florida Department of Insurance, and Florida Legislators have allowed this conduct to continue unabated for over twenty five years, to the point where every homeowner who files a claim believes he is going to be screwed. They are right. They are!

By their inaction, the Department of Insurance, and Florida Legislators have given tacit approval to the insurance industry of their current claims handling conduct; and they have been given a free ride and have turned a blind eye, with a wink and a nod, to all insurance companies' illegal and criminal conduct in the handling of claims, in flagrant violation of Florida statutes, for whatever reason you care to ponder.

Remember, those bulging, little brown envelopes are constantly becoming thicker, and spread further afield.

Perhaps, after these officials retire from Florida Government service, as "civilian" individuals they will be looking for a nice, cushy, highly paid job, probably with an insurance company, and perhaps in appreciation of services previously rendered. And then, maybe not. Maybe they are just lazy or incompetent, or just marking time until retirement.

The duty of finalizing the field adjuster's scope of loss falls to the desk adjuster who sits in the office, and "blue pencils" (deletes) any item he can delete with impunity, to save the insurance company more money.

If policyholders are unwilling to accept what the insurance company offers, their lives for any period of time between one year and seven or eight years become a waiting game, while the company uses all its resources to make its customers' lives a living hell. That is the reality in today's homeowner's insurance market.

And every year, the insurance department's civil servants continue discussions with insurance companies to determine how close to the legal limit of a rate/premium increase they can get to, which limit is currently set by Florida law at 10%.

All this goes on, while policyholders are still trying to get paid for the claim they made, how long ago?

If you walk away from your claim, your insurance company will be very happy, because their strategies and tactics will have succeeded, because they closed your claim file without making a payment.

The ultimate success story.

Working on the assumption that policyholders might wish to dig their heels in and sue their insurance company, policyholders should choose their attorney to handle their law suit carefully and wisely.

Policyholders filing suit against their insurance company should bear in mind that they need to sign up with an attorney who is knowledgeable and experienced in Florida property insurance law. Just because your cousin's nephew is a practicing attorney does not mean that he knows anything about Florida property insurance law, as a specialty from the plaintiff's perspective. He may be a Wills and Trusts attorney, and if so, and you hire him, your claim could be in serious trouble.

If you don't know an attorney, it is suggested that you should visit the website of the Florida Association of Public Insurance Adjusters, www.fapia.net. A high proportion of the attorneys practicing in Florida property insurance law, as plaintiffs' counsel, advertise on the website. All of them are top drawer, first class attorneys, and they will give you good advice.

And most of them will handle your claim under the terms of a standard, Florida Bar, contingency contract.

If a policyholder enters into a contract with an attorney on a contingency basis, the attorney will file suit and have the insurance company served with suit papers for breach of contract.

Once suit has been filed, even if the suit papers have not been served, the policyholders liability for his attorney's fees and costs are protected, by statute.

At the same time, the attorney will, probably, file what is called a Civil Remedy Notice (CRN). A CRN is a formal complaint filed with the Florida Department of Insurance recording that his homeowner's insurance company has violated several Florida statutes by improperly handling the policyholder's claim for a covered loss by using "Unfair Claim Handling Practices."

This is the first step towards filing a law suit against the insurance company for handling the policyholder's claim in "Bad Faith."

The filing of a CRN with the Florida Department of Insurance has two important functions:

1. The filing of a Civil Remedy Notice with the Florida Department of Insurance, gives notice to the Department that a formal complaint is being lodged against the insurance company named, for using "Unfair Claims Handling Practices" in the investigation and adjustment of a covered loss and claim.

Upon receipt of the CRN the department will issue what is called a "Letter of Acceptance," which records the official Date of Acceptance stated in the letter.

2. The Date of Acceptance is important to the process, because it starts a clock ticking for a period of sixty (60) days.

This period of sixty days is vital to the issue of the policyholder's complaint to the department of insurance for the following reason: The suit for breach of contract, before the Court, is running concurrently with the 60 day CRN notice to the Department of Insurance.

The insurance company, by Florida statutes, has a period of 60 days from the Date of Acceptance by the Department of Insurance of the CRN to "cure" (settle) the policyholder's claim.

If the insurance company settles the policyholder's claim, thereby "curing" the breach of contract, the claim against the insurance company will be dismissed by your attorney, With Prejudice, which means that the same claim cannot be re-filed at some future date.

Moreover, because the suit for breach of contract has "run its course" with the Court, the presiding Judge will dismiss that legal action, and will order the insurance company to pay the homeowner's attorney's legal fees and costs, at no expense to the policyholder.

However, if the insurance company ignores the CRN filed with the Department of Insurance, or lets the 60 day period to cure the breach of contract passes, without the breach being cured, two things happen.

1. The suit against the insurance company for breach of contract will continue through the court system to a conclusion either in favor of the plaintiff or the defendant.

2. If the suit for breach of contract by the insurance company concludes in favor of the policyholder plaintiff, whether by negotiation or an award by the Court, the policyholder now has what are called two "rights:" "A Right of Action" and a "Cause of Action," against the insurance company, meaning that the policyholder may now sue the insurance company

for handling his claim "in Bad Faith" if he, the policyholder, feels sufficiently aggrieved.

If the policyholder proceeds with filing suit against the insurance company for "Bad Faith," and he prevails, meaning that the jury finds in his favor, the policyholder will be awarded, "extra contractual damages" meaning damages "outside" of the insurance contract, for its Bad Faith conduct. Essentially, it is a punishment to the insurance company for dealing unfairly and illegally against its policyholder. Also, the plaintiff will be awarded his legal fees and costs of the "Bad Faith" action.

A WORD OF CAUTION: Some law firms do not protect the policyholder/client against a liability for his attorney's fees and costs which accrue in a breach of contract action.

Some attorneys, without discussing strategy or tactics with the policyholder/client, elect to try to negotiate a settlement between the policyholder and his insurance company. This can lead to the policyholder receiving a settlement, but then being liable for 30% or perhaps 40% of that settlement for his attorneys fees and costs.

After Hurricane "Wilma" I had a client, a law professor, who suffered a loss at his home. He was insured with Citizens Property Insurance Corp. and there arose a dispute relating to both the scope of loss and the quantum of the loss between my office and Citizens.

Negotiations reached an impasse, and I recommended a firm of attorneys to my client, who signed a contingency contract with that firm of attorneys.

Instead of filing suit, the attorney, without any consultation with my client, decided to try to negotiate a settlement with Citizens. After receiving a letter of representation from the attorney, Citizens threw in the towel and made a low balled offer of settlement, which the attorney then persuaded my client to accept.

Upon receipt of the settlement check from Citizens, the attorney charged fees against our mutual client at 40% as per the contingency contract.

I was so angry at this conduct, which I considered to be "sharp practice." that I refused to send my client an invoice for my services. He had paid enough out of pocket!

My client, being a gentleman (of the old school), insisted on paying my fee, and he pulled rank, reminding me that he was a law professor, and I was a public adjuster.

I dismissed his offer, and countered by reminding him that, in age seniority, I was at least ten years his elder.

We both had a good laugh, and he eventually said, "OK. You win"

I told the attorney, in no uncertain terms, that I would never recommend her firm again. And I never have.

However, I have referred many clients to other firms over the last ten years, and they have enjoyed my support to the tune of many hundreds of thousands of dollars in fees from those referrals.

Aside from the generalities otherwise noted in this guide, the largest homeowners' insurance company, in terms of premium income as at December 2017, *the one and only insurance company disciplined was Universal Property & Casualty Insurance Company of Fort Lauderdale, Florida* **which was fined by the Florida Department of Financial Services for "*Unfair Claims Handling Practices.*" The Department levied a fine of $1.26 million dollars, which I understand was negotiated down by Universal from a much larger amount.**

To insurers, particularly when they are the size of **Universal** , with an annual premium income approaching $1.0 Billion, this fine was a mere slap on the wrist.

Universal made (empty) promises to the Department of Insurance that it would stop its unfair and illegal claims handling practices, and then went straight back to doing exactly what it had been fined for doing, metaphorically thumbing it's nose at the Department of Insurance of the day.

Today, *Universal* continues its standard practices, using the McKinsey doctrine of Deny, Delay and Defend, "Unfair Claims Handling Practices" with continuing impunity, the current Commissioner turning his "blind eye" to their standard chicanery practices in the handling of claims.

It bears repeating, that one of the duties of the Florida Department of Insurance is to protect consumer policyholders from predatory insurers, using unfair and illegal claims handling practices, and operating a thinly disguised variation of a PONZI scheme.

Sadly, policyholders might just as well shout at the Atlantic Ocean, for all the shouting will fall on deaf ears.

We shall have to wait and see what the new Commissioner does in his term in office.

Don't hold your breath. Remember those bulging, little - well, you know what they are!

CHANGES IN CLAIMS HANDLING PRACTICES
SINCE McKINSEY'S DENY, DELAY AND DEFEND

Before McKinsey, insurance company staff adjusters, field adjusters and "independent" adjusters, for the most part, had a civil discourse with public adjusters. In those days, an insurance company's field adjuster was required to provide the insured policyholder(s) with a copy of his original estimate, which incorporated his original scope of loss, showing a line-by-line schedule of the work necessary to restore the insured property to its pre-loss condition, and showing also the line-by-line estimated quantities of materials and unit costs of each line item.

If a public adjuster was involved, the field adjuster's estimated was routed through the public adjuster.

If there was a material difference between the two estimates, the two adjusters met and sorted out their differences, and an agreement was reached, in accordance with the terms, conditions and limitations of the policy issued, and with full compliance with the applicable laws of the state in which the loss occurred. Finally, the claim was paid promptly and the file was then closed.

The system worked very well, for over a hundred years, since public adjusters representing the policyholder entered the market place.

Absent a public adjuster, the insured policyholder was treated fairly, and with professionalism.

This general claims handling system had worked very well for over four hundred years, since long before Edward Lloyd opened his coffee shop in the City of London, which welcomed mainly Master Mariners, intent on conducting insurance business, then a relatively "new" profession.

Today, because of the introduction to the market place by McKinsey of an adversarial and distinctly hostile and intentionally intimidating attitude towards all policyholders, who have had the misfortune to suffer a loss, the audacity to file a claim, let alone their perceived impertinence in hiring a public adjuster, new claims handling practices entered the market place.

Neither insurance company staff adjusters, field adjusters, nor any "independent adjuster" appointed by the insurance company to handle a claim, have any authority whatsoever to adjust the loss, and/or negotiate the claim with either the insured policyholder of the retained public adjuster, if one has been retained.

The insurance industry persuaded Florida's legislators (remember those bulging, little brown envelopes), to repeal the statute law which required the insurance company to provide their policyholder with a copy of the field adjuster's scope and estimate of loss.

Why did they do this. Simple!

With the advent of Deny, Delay and Defend, a strong possibility existed that if the policyholder were in possession of either a company or "independent adjuster's" scope and estimate, it would be far easier for plaintiffs' counsel to demonstrate that the insurance company was engaged in a rampant, day-to-day practice of defrauding policyholders.

So, what did the insurance companies do? they purchased protection from the Florida legislature.

Today, the insurance carriers' try to shield their estimate and other paperwork from discovery, labeling that documentation as semi-secret, "work product," and thus proprietary, and therefore privileged.

For the most part, those arguments have been debunked by the Courts because some documentation in a law suit is in the public interest to be disclosed.

As a result, insurance carriers' claims of "classified documentation" has fallen on deaf ears, as it should do.

As part of the McKinsey doctrine, the copy of the scope and estimate is only sent to the policyholder, as supporting documentation to a letter of offer of settlement, which also has attached to it, usually, a check, or draft in the amount of the offer to settle, probably around 10%/20% of the amount the insured is actually entitled to recover.

This is a clever move, because, as McKinsey argues, there is an all too common, human, psychological thought in the mind of the policyholder, which says, "Do I take the offer now (a bird in the hand is worth two in the bush), or do I hang in there to try to get more. If so, how long? and for how much more"?

At this stage the public adjuster has a meeting with his client. He knows that no useful purpose will be served by trying to negotiate those items which should be included in the estimate, by law. He will be told that "Management believes it is a fair offer."

The policyholder now has a decision to make. Does he accept the low-balled, short-changed offer of settlement, and walk away from the claim; or does he take the position that he doesn't care how long it takes, he wants 100% of his policy indemnity entitlement.

Many policyholders elect to take the money and run. They have had enough. And that is what the insurer is counting on.

A small percentage elect to go ahead with the law suit for breach of contract, accept the check as "undisputed funds" which, by Florida statute, insurers have to tender, or pay, within 90 days of the date of loss.

The issue of "Undisputed Funds" is dealt with, later in this guide.

As a third alternative, the policyholder might elect to demand Appraisal of the amount of the loss, which we discussed earlier.

The Appraisal should be capable of being completed with 60 - 90 days from the date the demand is made, but there is no guarantee that the process will work in the policyholder's favor, for reasons we explained earlier. It depends on whether the Umpire is genuinely neutral and impartial.

A law suit for breach of contract is a different matter. The insurance companies have become expert at creating delays during the process of, and the progress of the law suit through the system.

While it is unlikely that a claim would ever see the light of day in a Courtroom, the preparation and progress through the various steps towards trial continues with the highest level of fervor and aggressiveness they can muster. It is most likely that, with the help of an experienced plaintiff's attorney, the insurer will come to the negotiating table, but they would rather do so later rather than sooner, because the policyholder is likely to become more amenable to a solution, the longer he has to wait for settlement.

Frankly, the circuit court judges bear a certain degree of responsibility for the time it takes for a law suit to run its course.

Although there truly is a delay in setting a trial date because of the swarm of traffic on Court dockets and calendars, judges could make a serious impact on the progression to finality of a law suit if they would deny most, by which I mean 95% of defense requests for a continuance (rescheduling) of a matter to heard before the Court. Very rarely is there any genuine reason for a continuance. But it is an important procedure in the tactics of Deny, Delay and Defend, pursued by the insurer's defense team because if there is no real need for a continuance, to prolong the final resolution of a claim, the Court is being unfair to the Plaintiff. And Circuit Judges are elected, aren't they?

At a point in time, there comes a day, far ahead into the future, that the insured policyholder has his day in Court, where the issues are slogged out, not only between the attorneys when they stand before the presiding judge, but also the issues of law being argued before a largely lay jury. During such a Court hearing, seven or eight years after the date of loss, it often transpires that the memory of key witnesses may not be as precise as the attorneys on both sides would like to hear. Witnesses are human, not robots, and usually, when the witness is a public adjuster, he has dealt with hundreds, perhaps thousands of claims since the claim at issue, and it is impossible for him to recount with pin point accuracy precisely what he said to a plumber on a given day and time, eight years ago, on a claim which should have been settled and paid in three weeks.

At such a hearing, the insurer is well ahead of the game. The insurance company has earned probably 100% interest on the unpaid claim's eventual proceeds, bearing in mind their investments between the date of the loss and the date of trial, and by the time the insurer makes a payment, that payment is a net-zero payment.

Nevertheless, a law suit could take usually a minimum of two to three years to settle, although I have had many cases, using the right attorney, where a settlement has been achieved in two to three months.

And, of course, the insurer is going to be reimbursed, perhaps up to 90% or higher, of the claim's actual cost, plus attorney's fees and costs for both sides (plaintiff's and defendant's fees and costs), from its re-insurers, or a goodly proportion thereof depending upon the details of their applicable reinsurance treaties.

This is the exact time that the insurance company whines and bleats about the "high" level of legal costs which they have to absorb when handling a claim.

Always, they blame others.

The public adjuster, the plaintiff's attorney and plaintiff's contractors for those high costs, as ammunition to bolster their request to the Department of Insurance for a premium rate increase for the upcoming fiscal year.

When the time comes for the Department of Insurance to look at requests for premium rate increases each year, the Department's officials forget, or if they even know, that the insurer carries reinsurance, and is reimbursed for the "claims handling costs" by those re-insurers.

But, here is the quintessential issue.

The policyholder did not bring this claim on himself. In fact, the exact opposite is the case.

The insurers brought this situation on themselves and must bear one hundred percent of the blame for any and all negative consequences of their claims handling practices.

The policyholder is only seeking what the insurer promised, in their policies, in the event that the policyholder suffers a loss. The insurer decides, exclusively, on every claim, how they handle that claim.

The policyholder has no say on this issue at all.

The consequences of DENY, DELAY AND DEFEND, as a practice for handling claims **rests entirely upon the insurance company's shoulders**, and the policyholder has no choice other than to go along for the ride.

Moreover, nowhere in Florida statutes is it written that an insurance company, any insurance company, including Citizens Property Insurance Corporation, is entitled to demand that irrespective and any and all other considerations, they are entitled to make a profit.

Florida's insurance companies are not FPL. But that is another book, waiting to be written by someone else!

There is absolutely no reason whatsoever, why Florida insurance consumers should be asked to pay for the consequences of business decisions made by insurance companies' boards of directors.

Insurance companies make choices, as does every business, and the board of directors has to be accountable for its decision and actions.

To, the whiners I say this: "Quit the whining and bleating. Do your jobs and make your decisions, and live with the consequences."

So, you may not make a profit, or as much of an ill-gotten profit you have become accustomed to making by fleecing and by fraudulent means lining your pockets with your policyholders' money not as thickly as you have done in the past.

Florida's policyholders should demand, yes demand from its legislators, a total freeze on increases in premium rate increases, until Deny, Delay & Defend is sent packing, down the sewers of history.

CHAPTER 4

FLORIDA GOVERNMENT
OFFICE OF PROGRAM ANALYSIS & GOVERNMENT ACCOUNTABILITY

An independent office, FGOOPAGA, set up by the Florida Legislature was tasked, ten years ago, to investigate whether Florida's Licensed & Bonded Public Adjusters actually provided a valuable and necessary service to Florida homeowner consumers. That office reported, inter alia, thus:

PUBLIC ADJUSTER RETAINED

Non - Catastrophe Claims:

Percentage of **additional settlements**
achieved over original settlement offer   +574%

Catastrophe Claims (Hurricanes)

Percentage of **additional settlements**
achieved over original settlement offer   +747%

Typical Public Adjuster's Fees
Capped by Florida Statute:

Non - Catastrophe Claims   20%

Catastrophe Claims (Hurricanes)   10%

This independent report demonstrates the prudence of and benefits to the homeowner who hires a licensed & bonded public adjuster to handle his claim.

CHAPTER 5

INFORMATION AND COMMENT

Note: In 2004, I changed my Florida independent adjuster's license to a Florida, Public Adjuster's license ("All Lines" 3-20) allowing me to represent policyholders exclusively.

I made this change because of the then escalating practice by all insurance companies to change their traditional methods of handling claims, which I had used exclusively and very successfully for over fifty years, and switch to using the recommendations implicit in the McKinsey doctrine of "Deny, Delay and Defend."

This change in claim handling practices, I considered might be catastrophic in the long term.

Frankly, I could not, and would not condone, participate or support any policy of claims handling that required me to knowingly and enthusiastically, use practices that I characterized as being both dishonest and worse, illegal, and possibly, somewhere down the road as criminal conduct. I wanted no part of that scenario.

One afternoon, in 2004, I received a telephone call from an individual who described himself as the Regional

Property Claims Manager for State Farm insurance companies.

After introducing myself to him over the telephone, I asked him how I could help him.

He answered, "When are you going to stop writing these very nasty letters to my adjusters?"

I replied. "When your adjusters revert to paying claims as promised by your insurance policies, and the way you used to do prior to McKinsey coming upon the scene."

He said, "I haven't seen letters like these in twenty five years in the claims business."

I replied, "I haven't had to write them in fifty years in the claims business."

There was a long pause, and then he said, "Well, I guess we shall just have to disagree."

"Yes," I replied, "we shall."

With that he hung up his phone.

About fifteen minutes later, he called me again. I could tell he was now on a cell phone, probably speaking from his car.

He said, "HOW LONG have you been in the claims business?"

I replied, "Fifty years." another pause -

He then asked, "HOW OLD ARE YOU?"

I replied, "71!" - another - longer - pause.

And he said, "Well. Good luck to you, Sir."

I replied, "Thank you, Sir."

And we hung up.

I never heard from him again.

However, I should report that since that telephone conversation, I have had only one claim with State Farm where the McKinsey doctrine was used, which was a Hurricane "IRMA" claim, handled by a State Farm adjuster, a temporary import from Minnesota. In all the other claims I have had with State Farm, I have found their adjusters to be very professional, courteous, and knowledgeable, and claims have been settled promptly on all my State Farm claims, with that one exception, which is now in Appraisal. Claims were handled by the "Old School" rules which I found a most refreshing change, and I enjoyed working those claims.

My telephone conversation with the State Farm regional manager took me back to my youth, as a first day broker in the Underwriting Room, at Lloyd's of London, in the old, 1926 Lloyd's building on Leadenhall Street in the City of London.

I had been told by my boss, that until I knew someone in The Room very well, I should always address him as "Sir."

There were no ladies in The Room then. Today, there are many!

Within half an hour, on The Floor, I was introduced to the then, Chairman of Lloyd's. I addressed him as "Sir", and he addressed me back as, "Sir." And he wished me well.

He was maybe, 65 or 70 years of age.

I was 21. That's just the way it was.

CHAPTER 6

MISCONCEPTION BY
FORMER FLORIDA CABINET MEMBER

A Former Florida Cabinet Member, then head honcho at the Florida Department of Financial Services, Tom Gallagher, stated to an audience of perhaps three hundred people at a public meeting at a school in Fort Pierce, Florida, after one of the hurricanes of 2004, in answer to a question about hiring a public adjuster:

"No one needs a public adjuster. They just take money out of your pocket. Let your insurance company handle your claim, and you will be paid fairly."

After this remark by the then Secretary, effectively the Insurance Commissioner's boss, I felt compelled to challenge Secretary Gallagher with a letter, published in the South Florida Sun Sentinel, which I now paraphrase:

"A homeowner submitted a claim to his insurance company for damage to his home by a hurricane. The insurer's adjuster attended on site and wrote an estimate, and after the Deductible, the insured policyholder received a check for $4,000.00.

The homeowner was dissatisfied with this settlement and hired a public adjuster, who wrote an estimate, after the Deductible, for $40,000.00.

The public adjuster negotiated a settlement with the insurer, after Deductible, for $40,000.

The public adjuster achieved an additional payment for the policyholder of $36,000.00 which, after deducting his 10% fee, left the homeowner with $32,400.00 more than the amount for which the insurance company tried to settle. The public adjuster increased the recovery from the insurance company by 810% more that the insurance company paid originally.

Mr. Secretary, this scenario is common. How did the public adjuster take money out of his Client's pocket?

Secretary Gallagher did not respond to this question.

Obviously, his opinion was flawed, and self-serving and, moreover demonstrated (perhaps contrived for the occasion/planted question?), his profound ignorance of property insurance claims.

Former Secretary, Tom Gallagher, is now Chief Operations Officer at People's Trust Insurance of Deerfield Beach, Florida.

They deserve each other.

Enough said!

CHAPTER 7

PRESS PUBLICATION

The Huffington Post

By Molly Reilly & Max J. Rosenthall

December 13, 2011

Insurance Claim Delays Deliver Massive Profits to Industry by Shorting Customers

"*Washington - Unlike many other businesses, the insurance industry is bound by law to act in good faith with its customers. Because of the protective role in the lives of ordinary citizens, insurers have long operated as semi-quasi trusts. But, since the mid 1990s, a new profit hungry model, combined with weak regulation, has upended that ancient social contract.*

Claims have been converted into a money-making process, says Russ Roberts, a New Mexico-based management consultant and former business professor at Northwestern University, who had studied the insurance industry's evolution from a service industry to a profit driven machine.

The change started when consulting giant, McKinsey & Co. sold Allstate and other leading insurance companies on a new system to boost the bottom line. Rather than adjusting claims the traditional way, which gave claims managers wide latitude to serve their customers, insurers embraced a computer-driven method that produced purposely low offers to customers.

Those who took the low-balled offers received prompt service, while those who didn't had their claims delayed and potentially were reduced to bringing expensive law suits to fight for their benefits."

(In Florida, if you have to sue your insurers to get a claim paid, and you prevail in your law suit, the insurer pays your legal fees and costs).

CHAPTER 8

FLORIDA LICENSED ADJUSTERS

There are several classes of adjusters licenses issued to adjusters practicing of Florida.

Residents licenses are issued to adjusters who are permanent residents in Florida.

Non-Residents licenses are issued to those adjusters resident in another state who, mostly, are employed by a firm of adjusters who travel to Florida to assist insurers who are in need of temporary professional adjusters following a catastrophe, such as a hurricane.

The Resident Adjuster licenses are:

License 6-20 - Insurance Company "All Lines" Staff Adjuster.

This license is issued to a qualified adjuster, employed by an insurance company, either as a field adjuster, or an "inside desk" adjuster.

License 5-20 - "Independent" "All Lines" Adjuster.

This license is issued to a qualified adjuster who is either self-employed, or is employed by a firm of "independent" adjusters, and who is permanently resident in Florida, and who is employed either as a field adjuster or an "inside desk" adjuster or a "claims examiner."

NOTE: In Florida, the term "independent adjuster" is a misnomer. By definition, under Florida Statutes, he is *NOT* independent in the customary use of that term.

During discussions with any claims official employed by an insurance company they may point out that, if they assign a claim to an "independent adjuster," his Estimate will carry more weight with policyholders and other professionals, because he is "independent."

This is grossly misleading, and a classic misrepresentation typical of the attitude to claims handling practices by an insurance company in Florida.

By Florida Statutes, an "independent adjuster" may handle claims **ONLY** for (a) an insurance company, as a self-employed adjuster acting on an "ad hoc" basis on each individual assignment, and who is always subject to the insurance company's directions and claims handling practices; or he may work for a firm of "independent adjusters" employed by the insurance company to handle claims assigned to them by the insurance company, but he still takes "arms length" directions and claims handling practices from the insurance company's standard Claims Manual.

Notwithstanding the legal title in Florida statutes, there is no such individual who is truly "independent" in the normal, every day meaning of that term, as understood by "the man in the street."

3-20 - Public "All Lines" Adjuster

A Florida Licensed (and **Bonded**), and qualified "All Lines" Public Adjuster may be self-employed, or he may be employed by a firm of Public Insurance Adjusters.

He works exclusively for the policyholder, whose interests he is legally and morally duty bound to protect against the self-serving, **and illegal, DENY, DELAY AND DEFEND** claims handling practices used by insurance companies.

CHAPTER 9

PUBLIC INSURANCE ADJUSTERS

General Information

Presently, there are approximately 1,800 licensed and bonded, public adjusters resident in Florida, down from an all-time high of approximately 3,000 after hurricane "Wilma."

A very large percentage of the public adjusters now practicing in Florida were formerly senior or management adjusters who worked at some time for the insurance company/carrier side of the industry. But, became disenchanted with the then new McKinsey doctrine of claims handling practices spreading throughout the worldwide insurance industry like wild fire.

Essentially, they refused to be a party to deliberately short-changing policyholders, and misleading and/or misrepresenting policy coverages to policyholders, which they considered to be grossly dishonest and illegal practices, and which might possibly be determined to be criminal conduct at some time in the future.

FLORIDA ASSOCIATION OF
PUBLIC INSURANCE ADJUSTERS

In general, public insurance adjusters who are members of F.A.P.I.A. are vastly more knowledgeable, much better trained and experienced and, by attending continuing education conventions held in the state of Florida twice each year, are more up to date and more familiar with both Florida Statute and Case laws, which govern and set the standard for professional practices than are others who do not have access to those facilities.

Licensed, and Bonded, public insurance adjusters are the only advocates available to Florida homeowner policyholders, except attorneys, who abide by Florida law in the investigation, and adjustment of property claims, and who protect their homeowner clients' interests.

CHAPTER 10

DUTIES PERFORMED BY YOUR LICENSED
AND BONDED PUBLIC ADJUSTER

- Explains to the policyholder the terms and conditions of his contract with his insurance company.

- Explains to the policyholder the terms and conditions of his proposed Contract for professional services with the policyholder, which is required by Florida law.

- Provides the policyholder with a copy of the executed Contract of Representation.

- Writes a Letter of Representation to the insurance company, and proving them with a copy of his contract with the policyholder.

- Attends on site and inspects the insured property and makes detailed notes of any damage found, called the "scope of loss," including all hidden damage found, if any.

- Generates a detailed, line-by-line computerized Estimate of the costs of making good the damage and restoring the property to its pre-loss condition.

- Ensures that software is updated quarterly to reflect changes in prices of both materials and labor.

- Provides the policyholder and his insurance company with a copy of his completed Estimate with supporting documentation required either by the terms and conditions of the policy, and/or specifically requested by the insurance company/carrier.

- Contacts the carrier's field adjuster, and in liaison with the policyholder, arranges a joint meeting on site so that the field adjuster may make his own inspection, scope of loss and estimate.

- Meets the field adjuster on site, and if necessary, points out the areas of hidden damage.

- Assists the policyholder in preparing a Sworn Statement in Proof of Loss which, when signed and notarized, with become the policyholders' formal Statement of Claim, with supporting documentation, and photographs, as necessary.

- Submits the Sworn Statement in Proof of Loss to the insurance carrier. Explains any partial payment received by the policyholder from the insurance carrier and explains the Florida rules regarding the status of any "Undisputed Funds" element of that payment.

- Explains and discusses with the policyholder any omissions from the insurance company estimate, which should have accompanied the partial payment.
- Explains the options and makes recommendation as to the further action to be taken on the policyholder's claim.
- Attempts to negotiate a final settlement of the claim with the carrier.
- Explains the pros and cons of the binding Appraisal process and its alternative, non-binding Mediation.
- Discusses other options open to the policyholder.
- Establishes, if necessary, contact with the policyholder's attorney and briefs him on the essential issues relating to the claim.
- Provides the policyholder's attorney with a complete copy of his file, including photos, if any (on flash drive).
- Performs other duties, as directed by the policyholder's attorney, if any.

CHAPTER 11

PUBLIC ADJUSTER'S FEES

Public adjuster's fees are payable only after the policyholder has received payment(s) from his insurance company, whether they be partial payments, interim payment(s) or final payment(s).

The public adjuster is prohibited from charging any "out-of-pocket" expenses, such as telephone calls, copies, mail or courier services, etc. unless those charges are explained to the policyholder and are specifically spelled out in the public adjusters Contract of Representation, or an Addendum thereto, signed by both the policyholder and the public adjuster.

Public adjusters are prohibited by Florida statutes from charging any fees relating to checks received by the policyholder and dated prior to the date of the public adjuster's contract.

Public adjusters are prohibited by Florida statutes from charging any up-front fees under any circumstances.

Public adjusters are prohibited by Florida statutes from making any loans, cash advances, or any other gifts to a prospective client or a client under contract, having a monetary value (formerly $25.00), in excess of $100.00.

Finally, public adjusters fees are capped by Florida statutes, as follows:

Based upon claim payments received by the policyholder from, or on behalf of the insurance carrier:

Non-Catastrophe Claim Settlements   20%

Catastrophe Claims (Hurricane)
Settlements for the duration of a
declared period of a State of Emergency 10%

CHAPTER 12

INSURANCE COMPANY CLAIMS
HANDLING PRACTICES TODAY

The insurance industry no longer trains its field adjusters how to adjust a claim. That task is delegated to the company's claims estimating computer software, and their inside desk adjuster or claims examiner.

Nor do they inform, train or otherwise instruct their adjusters on existing Florida Statute laws, or Florida Case law, or changes in those laws, because to do so, would increase the amount of their bottom line payment, which in turn would be counter productive to the claims handling practices espoused by McKinsey.

Notwithstanding the McKinsey claims handling practices doctrine, insurance companies licensed to do business in Florida, **are compelled by Florida Statute law to include in their estimates those items which the statute states they MUST include in their estimates. This is not a requirement if they feel generous on a particular day.**

THEY ARE MANDATED BY STATUTE TO INCLUDE THOSE ITEMS.

Yet, in twenty-five years of ignoring these MANDATORY ACTION LAWS, NOT ONE SINGLE INSURANCE COMPANY EXECUTIVE HAS BEEN CALLED TO ACCOUNT, NOR BEEN SERVED WITH A SUBPOENA BY EITHER THE FLORIDA HOUSE OR THE FLORIDA SENATE TO APPEAR BEFORE EITHER BODY TO EXPLAIN WHY HIS INSURANCE COMPANY DISOBEYS THE LAW.

Not a single one, in twenty five years!

It's those bulging, little brown envelopes, again, and again, and again.

In insurance company claims handling practice, it is often the case that when a claim is filed, and the field adjuster makes his first inspection, the claim is denied by the company, with the stated reason being that the loss did not result from an "insured peril," or was caused by an "excluded peril" and is therefore, not covered by the policy.

The average "man in the street" would be amazed at the high percentage of claims in which this first denial is successful and the claim is not pursued.

This most often happens when a policyholder files a claim for a broken or collapsed water drain pipes under the monolithic concrete slab foundation of, let's say, the kitchen.

The insurance company's field adjuster attends on sight, inspects the house and the plumber's report and then declares that the loss resulted from wear and tear, which is an excluded peril under the policy. Indeed, he might even show the policyholder where in the policy, a loss caused by "Wear and Tear" is excluded.

Ninety nine times out of one hundred, the policyholder will say. "You are right. "Wear and Tear" is not covered by the policy."

The insurance company's field adjuster then returns to his office, tells his supervisor that the policyholder agrees that the loss is not covered by the policy, and the file is closed. His supervisor, says "Great Job!"

But, the actual costs of replacing the pipe may be minuscule in relation to the claim that is actually covered by the policy, which the field adjuster did not disclose.

What the insurance company's field adjuster did not tell the policyholder is that, whereas the policy does not cover the costs of replacing the collapsed section of pipe, the costs of accessing the broken pipe to facilitate the repairs to the pipe (including any and all damage caused to the insured property by this repair work), which may include jack hammering through the kitchen concrete slab, replacing the tile floors in the kitchen, and perhaps the entire house, if the tiles are laid a certain way, and pass through doorways and thresholds; and then the costs of replacing the upper and lower kitchen cabinets, with marble tops, all those costs are covered by the policy, which can total $60-70,000.00 or much more.

Most homeowner's policies in Florida have a "replacement cost" clause.

What is "replacement cost?"

"Replacement Cost" may be defined as:

"Replacement cost, with materials of like kind and quality, not better than, nor more extensive than, the original when new, without deduction for depreciation."

You will not find this definition in any insurance policy. But, it's Property Insurance 101.

Current law, in Florida, allows the insurance company to calculate a "depreciation factor" and hold back that amount from their settlement until such time as, within 180 days, the policyholder actually replaces the damaged items. When the work of repair has been completed, and the costs of actual replacement have been incurred, the policyholder may demand settlement of the depreciation factor withheld initially by the insurance company.

This time limit of 180 days is redundant if the claim is in suit for breach of contract.

The insurance companies have become masters at delaying the process of a claim, and the progress of a claim through the court system.

Of course they have! They have had twenty five years, free reign, to do exactly as they please, without a single government official calling them to account.

They fail to answer correspondence, or other paperwork for months, and then, when time is running out, they will pull the file from the law firm handling the defense of the claim, and assign the claim to another firm, so that the game of musical chairs starts all over again, from scratch.

I have a client, a corporation now owned by the original owner's widow, the original owner having passed away over two years ago, for a very minor drain pipe collapse claim at one of the corporation's rental homes.

Two months into the then new tenants' occupancy, water backed up in a drain pipe from a bathroom shower, and then into the commode which backed up and overflowed.

A plumber was called, who elected to re-route the drain pipe and avoid the cost of jack hammering through the bathroom floor, hallway floor and a bedroom floor slab to install new pipes. The insurance company, Citizens Property Insurance Corporation, because there was no water damage inside the house, denied coverage for this $12,000.00 +/- claim, being the actual cost of re-routing the new pipe to link up with the exterior plumbing lines, excluding the cost of the pipes.

Citizens Property Insurance Corporation assigned the defense of the claim to at least two firms, maybe even three firms of defense attorneys, during a period of seven years and still ongoing.

After seven years, and hundreds of thousands of dollars in attorneys fees, the matter was set down for a jury trial in Ft. Lauderdale, Florida in July, 2018.

This matter was settled, in a trial in favor of the policyholder, who was awarded $4,800.00 +/- plus attorneys fees and costs.

In order to re-route the new drain pipes, the plumber had to dig through a section of a "structure," **attached to the dwelling**.

The claim included an amount for damage to a structure **attached to the dwelling**.

The policy language covered the Dwelling described in the Declaration Pages, **including structures attached thereto.**

The closing argument by the defense firm was given to the jury by a lady of considerable experience, who deliberately **misrepresented to the jury** the coverage provided by the policy in her closing argument, and later **repeated that misrepresentation when the jury asked for clarification on that issue.** In quoting the language of the policy, **she read to the jury from the policy only that section of the coverage description that she wanted them to hear.** She omitted the language stating that the policy covered **"including other structures attached thereto."**

Defense counsel then compounded her deception to the jury, by further reading from the policy, only that part of the policy coverage on **"Other Structures'** that she wanted them to hear. In reading from the policy, she stated that there was $0.00 coverage for Other Structures under "Coverage B. " She was correct that there was no coverage for "Other Structures" but she omitted to quote the rest of the coverage sentence which in whole read "Other Structures, *separated from the dwelling by clear space.*

Thus, Counsel for the defense deliberately misrepresented the policy coverage to the jury, **first by omitting that coverage was included for other structures attached to the dwelling, and compounding** that deception by implying that there was no coverage for other structures by misquoting the lack of coverage applied to other structures, (only) separated from the dwelling by clear space.

I spotted this deception immediately, but could not do or say anything. I was sitting in the well of the Court.

Unfortunately, for the policyholder, neither the Judge nor Plaintiff's Counsel noticed the deception.

Thus, the jury in deciding on the amount to award to the Plaintiff, excluded the costs of repair to the "Other Structure, attached to the dwelling," believing that there was no coverage for that structure.

Needless, to say. After eight years, a win is still a win. And Plaintiff's counsel's fees and costs will be paid by Citizens.

Doubtless, the CEO of Citizens will continue to complain about legal costs of defending claims against contractors, legal counsel and public adjusters.

STOP PRESS: Defense Counsel have filed, after a jury verdict, a Motion for Summary Judgement of Dismissal and a Directed Verdict that the loss is outside the coverage provided by the policy.

The Court denied this motion.

In response, Citizens has now filed an Appeal with the Broward County Circuit Court.

I hope that, during the appeal to the Broward Circuit Court, that the issue of the damage to the **"Other Structure attached to the dwelling" will be re-addressed.**

Frankly, I was surprised by the misrepresentation by Counsel in her closing argument.

When I next see her, if I ever do see her again, I will remind her that integrity is like being "a little bit pregnant." There is no halfway.

CHAPTER 13

CITIZENS PROPERTY INSURANCE CORPORATION
PROTECTED BY FLORIDA STATUTES

Citizens Property Insurance Corporation, the second largest insurance company in Florida, by the number of policies in force in December, 2017, is one of the primary, and most aggressive, practitioners of the McKinsey claims handling doctrine of **DENY, DELAY AND DEFEND.**

Citizens claims handling practices, every day, and on almost every claim, are illegal, and in violation of all the Florida statutes relating to "unfair claims handling practices," to which, in theory, all insurance companies doing business in the state of Florida are obliged to respect and obey. All except one! Citizens Property Insurance Corporation is in a class all by itself. Why, because they are fireproof. They can do exactly as they please, with absolute and total impunity!

AND IMMUNITY! SOVEREIGN IMMUNITY!!

While all these Florida Statutes apply to all insurers doing business in Florida, including Citizens, there are no penalties specified in the statutes for ignoring these statutes, except to sue the offending companies, including Citizens, for breach of contract, and having prevailed in the underlying "breach of contract" action, suing the insurance company for "Bad Faith" conduct. But Citizens is immune from any liability for "Bad Faith" by its creating Florida statute. This immunity was included in their founding statute **"as a protection against law suits for "Bad Faith" filed by Florida citizens, in the public interest."**

Perhaps some law professor, somewhere, could explain that drivel to me.

These statutes are incredibly weak and of very little real value except that it keeps attorneys in business and also provides a forum for new attorneys at the Florida bar. A training ground if you like. They learn trial "know how" and Court procedures, but for the consumer clients are of little value, except that they provide a forum in which the cheated and low-balled claimant policyholder can obtain some redress.

As stated elsewhere in this guide, a short-changed policyholder can sue for breach of contract, and thereafter, after generally prevailing in the breach suit, can then go further, if they feel so inclined and sufficiently aggrieved, to then sue their insurer for "Bad Faith."

HOMEOWNERS INSURANCE GUIDE - FLORIDA 2018/19

The potential extra contractual liability applies to every insurer doing business in Florida, except Citizens.

Because Citizens is protected against actions for "Bad Faith" by its creating statute, and thus, they follow the McKinsey claims handling doctrine as a regular, daily method of doing business.

Why do they do this? Because they can, with the same frost free impunity that all insurance carriers doing business in Florida enjoy, when they are sued for breach of contract. There is no penalty, except liability for their policy coverages.

There are no consequences of any description, for "Citizens" at any level, except for breach of contract.

He who pays the piper calls the tune.

Secondary law suits in the property insurance market in Florida are rare. Most lawyers will not touch a "Bad Faith" case unless there is at least a million dollars in it for them to put "skin in the game." It is just not worth the effort and aggravation involved.

The Merlin Law Group, whose home office is located in Tampa, Florida, but who have offices in several other states as well as Florida, whose Founder and Senior Partner, William "Chip" Merlin is one of the leading

Page **99** of **209**

attorneys handling bad faith claims both in Florida and nationally.

One of the most important tenets, if not THE most important principle in the conduct of insurance business, going back to the very beginning of commercial insurance business over five hundred plus years ago, when master mariners met to conduct insurance business among themselves, more or less as a private club, was the principle of "Utmost Good Faith."

This principle epitomized every insurance transaction, and it meant that in all insurance contracts, there was the unspoken assurance that each insurer had the utmost, or highest confidence in the word and practices of the insured individual; and the insured individual had the utmost, or highest confidence in the word and practices of the insurer.

There is no greater trust one can have, each in the other, beyond **utmost good faith.**

In recent times, largely because of the actions and practices of those insurance companies following in the footsteps of McKinsey, the principle of "Utmost Good Faith" has been diluted, and the word "Utmost" has been virtually eliminated from insurance language by practice and ill-gotten custom, from the meaning of the principle in the non-marine insurance marketplace.

"Utmost Good Faith" was a far higher level of good faith, than simple "Good Faith." So, now, we just have good faith, which means, apparently, and by judicial ruling by the Florida Supreme Court, that personal and commercial habits and practices of conducting insurance business, does not imply any integrity in the word or practices, each of the other, any more. According to the Justices of the Florida Supreme Court, if you can do something which used to be taboo, to make a buck. Good for you. Welcome to the current real world.

Because we now deal with each other, only in good faith, meaning without any real integrity, and with my fingers crossed behind my back, is the norm. And it shows in our daily lives, not only in the insurance industries, world wide, but in our day-to-day lives we lead, and those we encounter and perhaps do business with, on our journey through life.

There is one caveat to my last comment.

As far as I know, but certainly in the European insurance marketplace, the practice and understanding of the expression **"Utmost Good Faith" is still the standard for customs and practices in the marine market**, in which I have not practiced seriously since I changed my license from "Independent" to "Public" in

2004. Frankly, there is little need or demand for a public adjuster in the marine insurance marketplace.

I wish it were so in the non-marine marketplace, but we have to play the game with the cards we are dealt, and make the best of what we have.

Citizens hides behind the cloak of immunity from law suits for bad faith in its claims handling practices, again, because it can.

Citizens CEO enjoys his position, and actively encourages claims employees to short its policyholders' claims. For his entire senior management career, he has been an enthusiastic supporter proponent of the McKinsey doctrine of claims handling practices.

Perhaps, one of these days, Florida's legislators will see the error of their ways by repealing the "immunity from Bad Faith" clause contained in Citizens founding statute, and level the playing field. By doing so, accountability, and the restoration of full right to Florida policyholders will occur, and moreover, will give Florida policyholders the protection of the "equal protection clauses" in both the Florida and the United States Constitutions. This action would force Citizens to acknowledge that, for every action, there is an equal and opposite reaction.

Citizens, of course, is a "not for profit" Florida corporation, so why does it matter to them if they cross the line between fair and reasonable claims handling practices and dishonest, and illegal, claims handling practices?

Because, although Citizens is a "not for profit" corporation, its CEO is still answerable to the Florida government for its business performance, year by year.

Exactly the same position existed behind the Iron and Bamboo Curtains, in what used to be the USSR and China during the Communist regimes of yesteryear, and where in a previous life I handled multiple claims for the multinational insurers. In those systems of government, profit was a dirty word. However, while every business was government owned, every business manager was accountable to his Comrade Management Executive Board for the performance of their businesses.

Thus, while they never made a "profit," they were always at pains to make a "Surplus."

Citizens, therefore is expected by its overseers to make a surplus, and its CEO tries to see that it does so, every year. But, having a surplus, however obscenely large, does not stop Citizens from asking for a rate (premium) increase, almost every year.

For example, in its 2016 year of account, Citizens Underwriting Account had a premium income of almost $1Billion dollars, actually, $973,840,305. Total claim payments were $344,926,118, producing a surplus of $628,914,187 with which to run its business administration, and contribute to its Reserves.

Yet, this massive level of surplus in its underwriting account did not stop Citizens from asking for a rate/premium increase to bolster its underwriting account revenue, pleading higher than anticipated claims handling costs. **Seriously?**

I am not an accountant, but I have to comment that I have a strong feeling that "All is not well in the State of Denmark!"

I sense that Citizens is a bloated bureaucracy, with a large excess of unnecessary management personnel at its middle to top management levels. Just a thought.

The "failure to act in "Good Faith" in the handling of a policyholder's claim by Citizens reached the Florida Supreme Court, where the suit was dismissed, on the grounds that the matters alleged against Citizens in a claim by one of its policyholders, San Perdido Condominium Association, technically, did not reach the level of "willful tort" which is one of the exceptions to immunity to Citizens for its actions against its policyholders in its claims handling practices.

It is generally accepted, in the English speaking world, and thus where the English language is spoken as a "first language," that a "willful tort" is a deliberate and intentional act/action taken by one entity or person against another entity or person which causes harm to that (victimized) entity or person, and which thus, is actionable. The possibility of an actual "willful tort" without a means of redress is absurd.

I am sure the "Ordinary Man in the Street" would view Citizens antics in the handling of San Perdido, being that those intentional actions were **THE VERY ESSENSE OF, AND AT THE VERY CORE OF THE McKINSEY CLAIMS HANDLING PRACTICES AND DOCTRINE**, should be self-evident to any reasonably well educated person who had bothered to read the case, including the Florida Supreme Court Justices.

Perhaps, the Supremes in Tallahassee should experience, first hand, the filing of a claim with Citizens, the object being better to understand what is, and what is not, a "willful tort," to the average "man in the street."

What on Earth were the Florida Supremes thinking? and what were they smoking? and which English speaking planet are they from?

Someone once said, "Common sense is not always common." How true!

Mr. Bumble, in Oliver Twist said, "The Law is a Ass!" Also, so true. But, it's not only "The Law!" Sometimes, it applies to those who practice law, through rose tinted glasses, and/or perhaps with their own agenda?

I invite any of the "learned justices" on the Florida Supreme Court to spend two days in any public adjuster's office, or an office of a plaintiffs' attorney's practice. They would very soon better understand the true meaning of "willful tort" to the average "man in the street," which would be any Florida policyholder with a claim against Citizens, or any other insurance homeowners' insurance carrier trading in Florida. Experience the joy of "willful tort" in the real world!

However, in fairness, notwithstanding my criticism of Citizens in its claims handling practices, I have to report that, artificial or not, I have detected a change in the way Citizens has handled claims arising out of the passage north, through Florida of Hurricane "IRMA" which crossed the Florida coast on September 10, 2017.

On the "IRMA" claims I have handled, for returning clients and referrals, which are the only claims I now accept in semi-retirement, where Citizens is the insurance carrier, I have found, with only one exception, that Citizens field adjusters to be very professional, and fair and reasonable in the writing of scopes of loss and subsequent estimates, and reasonably prompt settlements (which has been a refreshing change from the "smell of the pit" which is the Florida claims market place), and almost, but not quite, back to the old method of handling claims, prior to McKinsey.

I hope, very sincerely, that Barry Gilway has seen the light, and that this is a step back to correcting some of the more odious conduct and practices of most individuals involved in the first party, property claims markets both in Florida and worldwide.

It just takes one individual, with authority, influence and vision (even if it's vision through the rear view mirror), to get the ball rolling.

We shall see.

CHAPTER 14

ASSIGNMENT OF BENEFITS

This guide would not be complete without a discussion on this topic, which has caused a great deal of comment in the South Florida print and other media, in the recent past, most notably by the CEO of Citizens, and others at executive levels of other insurance companies.

In my opinion, many of their comments, if true, have merit, but some of the problems seem to have a degree of self-serving deliberation about them, mostly from non-insurance professionals, who are taking advantage of a situation made worse by putting their tongues in their cheeks, and manufacturing difficulties where none need exist, to meet their own agenda.

The assignment of benefits issue, apparently, often arises after an insured has suffered a serious water damage loss. Out of dire necessity, the homeowner calls a water extraction company, and/or a plumber who attend promptly on site, perhaps in the middle of the night. Before any work is commenced, the homeowner is required to sign a Contract for Professional Services to be performed, while the offending water intrusion to the property is continuing. The policyholder feels that he has few options. He needs to get emergency work started

HOMEOWNERS INSURANCE GUIDE - FLORIDA 2018/19

immediately, and thus, he signs the contract, as a pro-active effort to comply with his policy conditions, which require him to take necessary action to mitigate the loss.

The contractor explains to the homeowner that they will take care of everything to get the necessary emergency work done, and he will bill the insurance company direct. This seems to be the answer to the homeowner's immediate problem. However, rarely does the homeowner/policyholder know what his insurance policy covers and/or requires him to do, and so he is thankful that the contractor will do what work is necessary on an emergency basis, and since the contractor will bill the insurance company direct, he is relieved at not having to make a trip to a bank to withdraw cash, or, in the middle of the night, visit an automatic teller machine.

He believes that he has nothing to worry about.

However, included in the contract with the water extraction contractor is what is called an **"ASSIGNMENT OF BENEFITS"** clause which stipulates that, as surety for being paid for his professional services, the contract provides *that all the rights to the benefits owed to the insured policyholder by the insurance company are transferred to the contractor.*

This seems, at first sight to the homeowner, to be

a perfect solution, and all his worries will go away, and he signs the contract.

But, this is when the problems start.

The policy issued to the policyholder states that, if he suffers a loss which will give rise to a claim under the policy, there are certain duties imposed upon the policyholder with which he _**MUST**_ comply, to protect both the rights of the insurance company, and the policyholder's rights to benefits under the policy.

The policy contains no language which explains these mandatory duties to the policyholder. He is expected to know what the language of the policy means, and if, for any reason, he fails to comply with his mandatory duty, the insurance company has the right to deny the claim.

If the policyholder fails to act as he required to do by the mandatory duties imposed upon him by the policy, and the insurance company places him on notice that they may have a right to deny coverage for the loss, the policyholder has a very serious problem on his hands.

If coverage for his claim is denied, there will be no transferred benefits (monies) payable to the contractor by the insurance company, under his contract with the contractor.

This may then lead to the contractor filing a contractor's lien on the insured property, which, if matters continue to escalate out of control, may result in foreclosure proceedings being started by the contractor against the homeowner/policyholder.

Before we go further, let us think about this situation.

Unfortunately, because the homeowner is most often not an individual schooled in the technicalities of the insurance contract, he is very quickly out of his depth.

He does not understand his duties under the policy, and innocently and without any intention to create problems for himself, the contractor or the insurance company, he discovers there are very serious problems.

Under his contract with the policyholder, the contractor had no duty to contact the insurance company. His contract only transfers money owed to the policyholder, by the insurance company, to him. Any problems the policyholder may have with his insurance company are not his concern. He only wants to be paid.

The insurance company, we are given to understand, by press and other published media statements, very often know nothing about their insured policyholder's loss and claim, until a contractor's invoice is presented to the insurance company for the services rendered to their policyholder, and asking to be paid the amount shown on the invoice for services rendered.

It is now necessary to explain to the policyholder exactly what his duties are, when he suffers a loss.

The language of the insurance policy issued to the policyholder contains certain language which the policyholder needs to understand.

One of these "matters" fall under the policy language called the **CONDITIONS.**

These CONDITIONS impose certain duties upon the policyholder, and the action(s) he _MUST_ take to comply with the Conditions to protect his position under the policy. As stated earlier, if he fails to comply with a CONDITION, for any reason, he is placing his entitlement to policy benefits at risk of denial of his claim.

Included in these **SECTION 1 - CONDITIONS** is a paragraph, or language, which states, in heavy type letters:

YOUR DUTIES AFTER LOSS

or words to that effect.

These duties, which I cannot emphasize enough are actions you *MUST* take to protect your position under your policy.

The language of the policy states:

"**Your Duties After Loss.** In case of a loss to covered property, you must see that the following are done:

a. Give **prompt** notice to us or our agent;

d. Protect the property from **further damage**.

If repairs to the property are required, you must:

(1) Take **reasonable and necessary** steps to protect the property; and

(2) Keep an accurate record of repair expenses;

f. As often as we require:

(1) Show us the **damaged property;**

(2) Provide us with records and documents we request and permit us to make copies; and

(3) Submit to examination under oath, while not in the presence of any other "insured" and sign the same;

Most homeowner's insurance policies in Florida include, on Page 1, a list of **Definitions.**

There are no definitions for the expressions: "**prompt**," "**further damage**," "**reasonable and necessary**" or "**damaged property**."

Since there are no definitions shown in the policy against these expressions, Florida Courts have held that these expressions mean what the "**average man in the street**" thinks they mean.

To further confuse the issue, the expression "**average man in the street** thinks they mean" is not defined in the policy, either!

Several Bills were considered in the 2018 legislative session, but none of those bills were seriously considered for being brought to the floor of either the House or the Senate, and the status quo remains stuck in a quagmire of meaningless vague statements and ambiguity, and in the hands of either incompetent or ignorant legislators, or individuals with their own agenda.

Florida is a multi-cultural state. Thus, if insurers really want to avoid controversy and potentially expensive attorneys and possibly law suits, the industry has to toughen up, bite the bullet and "spell it out" so that everyone can understand what it is they are obliged, by a **condition**, to do when they suffer a loss.

1. What is "prompt" notification?

One proposal, in 2018, in the Florida house, suggested that a homeowner should notify the insurer of a loss likely to result in a claim be "notified to the insurance company **within seven days after the completion of permanent repairs**. This suggestion was pure insanity, and demonstrated that its author had zero understanding whatever as to how insurance claims are supposed to work, and have worked for centuries.

To the average West Indian, **"prompt"** could mean (and I intend no offense), something close to, **"within a week or ten days, maybe, if I get to it."**

Solution: New claims should be notified to the insurance company **immediately** the damage is discovered, or, at the very latest, within twelve (12) hours of the discovery of the loss.

Under the traditional system of claims handling practices, for example, a burst/failed/leaking water pipe, supply line or drain line, was reported to the insurer (the next call after the first call to a plumber), certainly, within 12 hours, and an adjuster was assigned to attend on site that same day. That adjuster would inspect the damage, determine its cause, determine if that cause of loss was covered by the policy and authorize what emergency repairs could be carried out by the plumber, and arrangements were made for a further inspection by the company adjuster (of the completed (?) temporary repairs), and to agree with the contractor and the insured a date a time for the next appointment, on site, probably the next day, to discuss and authorize the scope and level of the permanent repairs which could start immediately after that second meeting.

Today, because insurance companies have withdrawn all authority from adjusters to make any decisions, except a denial of coverage, there is confusion and/or stalemate.

Today's situation **MUST** change. An insurance company notified of a water damage loss must have an adjuster on site that same day. **It is not rocket science, and "prompt" notification of loss could and should be properly explained in the policy, in plain, every day English language to avoid any misunderstandings.**

2. What does "protect the property from further damage mean?

a. Turn off the water at the main water supply valve to the insured property.

b. Place towels, sheets and other material that will soak up, and/or act as a dam against the onward progress of the water to other areas.

c. Call a water extraction company. Check with the plumber, he will be able to give you a name and telephone number.

3. What does "reasonable and necessary" mean?

If the kitchen sink faucet breaks in the middle of the night, and you do not discover that failure for, perhaps three hours, then obviously you have a problem.

You, as the homeowner, should know where the main, water shut off valve is located. In Florida is usually located in the front yard of the house, and it needs either a purpose built key to turn off the water, or if you do not have a key, a large plumber's adjustable wrench might get the job done.

Let us suppose that you have been able to turn off the water, but the first floor of you house is flooded, and carpets, floor coverings etc. are damaged.

Let us suppose, also, that your wife has called a water extraction company, and they are on their way to your home.

It is **"reasonable and necessary"** for them, having extracted as much water as they can from the home, to remove the wet carpets, and padding from the home and stack it by the edge of your property for disposal later.

Let us also suppose that your wife, knowing you are busy with other things, has taken over 100 photographs on her cell phone, of the damaged interior of the home, including the removal of the carpets, padding etc. from the home, and including the stacking of the ruined carpets now lying at the edge of your property waiting for disposal.

Let us suppose, also, that neither you, as the homeowner, nor your wife as the housekeeper of the home are in the kitchen drinking a cup of coffee made with bottled water, when you hear the bulk garbage pick-up truck service rolling up to the front of your home, and their frontend loader has picked up the carpets and padding and are on to their next call. You have nothing but the photographs to show the insurance company the extent of the damage to the carpets and padding.

You have nothing to worry about. The insurance company would, or should, understand your predicament and will agree with you that you did what was "reasonable and necessary," under the circumstances.

4. What does "show us the damaged property mean?"

This means exactly what it says. The adjuster for the insurance company has a right, on behalf of and as the representative of the insurance company, to see the **DAMAGED PROPERTY, meaning the/that part or section of the plumbing system that failed, and the damage to your property that the pipe failure caused.**

If the failed pipe, valve or other part of the plumbing system that failed has been repaired as a temporary and/or emergency, semi-permanent or permanent repair, keep the damaged or failed items for the adjuster to see, and if necessary, for technical reasons (subrogation, perhaps), take possession of the failed and/or damaged valve, or whatever, and take photographs for your file.

The homeowner, if he has the necessary facilities, even a cell phone, to take photographs, take as many photographs as you can, and provide copies of those photographs to the insurance company's adjuster.

One of the major problems that an insurance company has with water damage claims is, or so we are led to believe, that plumbing repairs have been completed, including damaged or collapsed underground pipes have been replaced, and the old damaged pipes have been disposed of, before the insurers have been placed on notice of a loss. The first indication they often receive is an invoice for services rendered to a policyholder.

This causes a very serious, major problem.

No homeowner, no plumber and no water extraction contractor would think of buying a home, sight unseen, or even diagnosing a cause of loss without having sight of the damaged property.

To protect its interests, therefore, the insurance company is entitled to **SEE the DAMAGED PROPERTY**, and the Condition seeks to give them that authority.

If the insurance company is denied that right, then it is unreasonable for them to be expected to pay a claim, virtually sight unseen.

Their interests have clearly been prejudiced by them being unable to verify the loss, the cause of loss, the scope of loss and therefore, to determine from an investigation that a covered loss has occurred.

Under these circumstances, the insurer has every right to rely on the Conditions in the policy, and deny coverage for the loss.

SUMMARY
ASSIGNMENT OF BENEFITS

An explanation of your obligations to your insurance company under the "Your Duties After Loss" section of the "Conditions" requirement of your policy will never fit all possible scenarios.

However, notwithstanding that, under the McKinsey doctrine of claims handling practices, your insurance company would prefer not to pay you anything, that does not mean that under certain circumstances, they cannot avoid a justifiable claim, nor does that mean that they are going to "go easy" on you.

They will still try to make sure that your claim is low-balled relative to the amount you are actually entitled to recover under your policy. The greater the loss, the greater the necessity for you to have a competent and experienced public adjuster standing in your corner, and looking after your interests.

There are a thousand and one ways the insurance company's computers can short-change, and scam you out of every penny they can. And they will do so if you give them half a chance.

An "Assignment of Benefits" clause is included in almost every contract presented to you for your signature by water extraction contractors, and/or plumbers.

If your need for either a water extraction contractor, or a plumber is a true emergency, then you may have no other option available to you.

The main problem for the consuming homeowner, policyholder is that while the contractor has enjoyed the transfer of policy benefits to his account by the terms of his contract, custom and practice, the contract places no obligation on the contractor to do anything to protect your interests under your policy.

In my opinion, at the very least, the Florida legislature should find a way to require the inclusion in policy language that, if policy benefits are transferred to a contractor to protect the contractor's interests, then the policy should require the contractor to assume also, the obligatory "duties after a loss" imposed upon the homeowner by his policy. By so doing, the contractor would be bound to protect both the policyholder and the insurer. And, if the contractor, for whatever reason, prejudices either the policyholder's interests under his policy, or the insurer by failing to protect their respective interests by complying with the assumed "duties after loss," then the contractor would be liable to either the policyholder for breach of contract, and/or the insurer, on a subrogation basis.

Faced with this obligation, I suspect that most contractors, both water extraction contractors and/or plumbers would delete the Assignment of Benefits clause from their contracts.

FLORIDA SUPREME COURT DECISION

Recently, the Florida Supreme Court was asked to weigh in on the "Assignment of Benefits" issue in contractors' contracts.

In short, the Court held, that the right to assign benefits under a Florida homeowner's policy, to whosoever the assignor wishes, has become an established custom and practice in the marketplace, which it was not going to disturb.

However, the Court went on to say that the more appropriate forum in which to resolve this issue would be in the Florida Legislature, and not in the Florida Court system.

Yes! Well, we have all witnessed the backbone and caliber of our legislators. Again, remember those bulging, little brown envelopes.

POST SCRIPT
ASSIGNMENT OF BENEFITS
REFORM SUGGESTIONS

There are some suggestions I would like to make to try to break the break the stalemate that now exists on this issue.

- Consideration might/could be given to replacing the existing Assignment of Benefits clause with a separate Contract incorporating an:
- "( ) Emergency Services Notification", and/or
- "( ) Emergency Repairs Notification," and/or
- "( ) Permanent Repairs Required Notification",
- which would require the contractor to email a copy of his Contract with the policyholder to the insurer within the same calendar day upon which the emergency service was provided at the insured premises, that document to be signed by both the policyholder and the contractor.

   This form could be in the "First Notification of Loss" to the insurer.

- Included in the "First Notification of Loss", and under the heading of "Emergency Services" the insurer would be advised of brief details of the emergency work completed to date, which would be signed by the policyholder and the contractor.

- The contractor's Emergency Services Invoice, not to exceed the amount of the policyholder's deductible, could be attached to the "First Notice" or could be emailed to the insurer within three calendar days of the date emergency services were performed. Again, the invoice would be signed by both the contractor, and the policyholder.

- Checks and/or drafts would list the named payees as 1. The policyholder, 2. The contractor and 3. Any other person or entity required to be included.

- Settlement of the invoice for the Emergency Services performed to be made within seven (7) business days of submission to the insurer.

- The contractor would be required to submit a proposal for any permanent repairs required, with a firm and definitive estimate of costs, with any changes to be made by a Change Order, signed by both the contractor and the policyholder, and emailed to the insurer within three business days of the date emergency repairs were performed; Approval of the estimate for permanent repairs net of any adjustments, within seven calendar days of submission to the insurance carrier.

- Payment for any permanent repairs necessary would be made by the insurer, against an Invoice dated within seven days of completion of a satisfaction note signed by both the contractor and the policyholder.

These steps would satisfy the policy requirements for prompt notification of loss; limit the immediate work to emergency repairs, not to exceed the deductible, and enable the insured policyholder and the insurer to control the claim, while at the same time guaranteeing timely execution of repairs and payment of both emergency repairs and permanent repairs, if any.

I anticipate that the parties to this issue would argue ad infinitum, and nit-pick about everything.

But this might just be a seed which might generate at least a start to serious and objective discussions on the issue. The present system gives contractors far too much control over the claim, and often leaves the policyholder trying to understand why and how he was thrown under the bus, by a contractor who only has his own interests to consider.

CHAPTER 15

THE FLORIDA LEGISLATURE

Our Florida Legislators have finished another of their boondoggle, annual trips to Tallahassee, to do God only knows what, apart from ensnaring those bulging, little brown envelopes which have become so large a part of their favorite lobbyists lives, which we all recognize, and which are euphemistically referred to as "contributions to their re-election campaign funds."

Yet again, it seems that the insurance industry, neither insurer nor consumer policyholder, had anything material to write home about this year. The status quo continues to become more and more bloated and unabated, and it never seems to change.

The 2018 legislative session will go down in history as yet another, utter, total, waste of time and money.

Status Quo! Yes. Indeed!

CHAPTER 16

OPTION TO REPAIR
(CONFLICT OF INTEREST)

The Option to Repair is, by far, the most insidious and duplicitous clause I have ever seen, in any insurance policy anywhere in the world.

The Option to Repair clause is now appearing in Florida policies, as a **CONDITION** most particularly in policies issued by **People's Trust Insurance Company of Deerfield Beach, Florida, and Heritage Insurance Company of Sunrise, Florida.**

Peoples Trust are now suing some of their policyholders, because those policyholders object very strongly into being tricked into accepting a clause which they did not fully understand, and which neither **People's Trust nor their agent(s)** explained properly to them, when they applied to the company for coverage.

The first problem that arises out of the **People's Trust** issue, is that the **Option to Repair clause** is written into their policy as a **CONDITION** (See Chapter 15), which obligates the policyholder to allow **Peoples Trust** to completely **"take over" their claim, and stand in the policyholder's shoes,** when their policyholder suffers a loss which leads to a claim under the policy, making all decisions as to the substance of the claim, and the method(s) to be used in making the repairs? who does the repairs? are the contractors workers' qualified? and what is their immigration status?

Moreover, the **"Option to Repair" Condition**, it must be emphasized, gives absolute and total control over all aspects of the Insured's claim, including giving People's Trust's affiliated company, Rapid Response Team, Inc. full access to the premises, even if the premises are temporarily unoccupied, and/or when no-one is temporarily at home.

There is a clause in People's Trust's Application for a Homeowner's Insurance Policy, which People's Trust describes as an "Optout" clause. But this "Optout" clause is not explained to prospective policyholders by the insurance company's agent(s), nor are those prospective policyholders advised of the affect the "Option to Repair" clause will have on any claim they submit to the insurance company.

People's Trust recently issued a statement to the print and other media, that if an applicant for homeowner's insurance signed the "Optout" clause in the application for insurance, the application **would be rejected. They did not want that applicant's business.**

As stated in Chapter 15, a breach of a Condition in the policy makes the claim voidable at the insurance company's option, and is an absolute defense to coverage.

However, there is another issue which I believe is far more important, to policyholders who have policies issued by People's Trust.

In the **Assignment of Benefits** issue, covered in Chapter 15, the benefits payable to the policyholder were assigned to the contractor employed to provide certain professional services.

In the Option to Repair clause, those same rights are surrendered TO PEOPLES'S TRUST, as the insurer.

Thus, by the terms and conditions of the policy issued by People's Trust to its policyholder, it has taken over total control of the policyholder's claim, while at the same time, having total control over its affiliate company, Rapid Response Team.

There is yet another issue:

People's Trust, has a fiscal duty to its policyholders, but by also having control over its contractor, Rapid Response Team, while, at the same time, having taken over total control over the insured policyholder's claim People's Trust has created a *MASSIVE THREE WAY*

CONFLICT OF INTEREST which it is barred from acquiring by Florida Statutes.

WHAT WERE THE OFFICIALS THINKING AT THE FLORIDA DEPARTMENT OF FINANCIAL SERVICES, DEPARTMENT OF INSURANCE, TO ALLOW THIS CLAUSE TO BE INSERTED IN THE POLICY, which is not only a violation of several Florida Statutes, but a violation of both the FLORIDA CONSTITUTION, and the CONSTITUTION OF THE UNITED STATES.

It would be nice, and the right thing to do, for the suits against People's Trust policyholders to be dismissed, **With Prejudice**, and the **Option to Repair** clause to be declared null and void, as a **conflict of interest, and thus, unenforceable and, incidentally, not in the public interest.**

Moreover, by acting as insurer and contractor, and by kidnapping also the policyholders' rights over their claims, People's Trust is actively engaging in a barely disguised, variation of a PONZI scheme, and racketeering.

Governor Scott, how about suspending People's Trust's license to do business in the State of Florida, and appointing a special prosecutor to inquire into People's Trust and it's tentacle companies.

Oops! I forgot: You were convicted of Medicare Fraud when you were CEO of a health care organization, and you only avoided serving prison time by "Pleading the Fifth" against self incrimination.

But you were fined $1Billion.

You obviously have a close fellowship with the insurance companies. Oh, well, screwed again!

And who is the Chief Operations Officer at People's Trust? Tom Gallagher!

Birds of a feather...........................

If you are a People's Trust policyholder, I have a suggestion for you:

CANCEL YOUR POLICY. TODAY - NOW!!

And get a full pro-rata return of your premium, and replace your homeowner's insurance with another carrier.

See Chapter 20.

CHAPTER 17

SUMMARY OF DENY, DELAY AND DEFEND

The caliber, and mind set of insurance company executives managing insurance companies today has changed since our parents' days.

Today, put quite simply, these individuals for the most part, are merely opportunists, and by their own actions demonstrate that they are individuals without character, ethics or integrity. Their only purpose is to scam as much money as they can from unsuspecting homeowners, and use their insurance companies as a tool to separate as many individuals from their hard earned money as they can, and to keep as much of it as they can by obfuscating on legitimate claims using extreme means; by massively underpaying claims when they have to make a settlement, without any fear of being called to account by any Florida government authority.

Many of the major "players" in the "rookie" homeowners' insurance companies are unscrupulous carpetbaggers who had never been in the insurance business until the wholesale, hysterical flight of the established insurance companies from Florida after Hurricane Andrew in 1991; and later, the multiple hurricanes of 2004, and 2005 which opened up an opportunity to join the bandwagon created by McKinsey.

Essentially, they realized that the insurance laws in Florida were weak (and remain so today), and Florida legislators, weaker, and without any backbone and easily manipulated.

Those bulging, little brown envelopes!

They took advantage of the moment of opportunity and ran, hot foot, to Tallahassee, to form their cardboard insurance companies.

They realized, very quickly, that they were sitting on a gold mine.

They took to McKinsey's doctrine of Deny, Delay and Defend like ducks to water, and the Florida regulators and legislators drank their "Kool Aid" by the gallon, like drunken sailors. The "New Boys" just could not believe their good fortune.

The result is a plethora of unscrupulous insurance companies, most of whom will disappear overnight after the next really destructive hurricane comes Florida's way, having far exceeded their PMLs. (Probable Maximum Losses), and go belly up.

Many of the rookie insurance companies are reminiscent of flaky, but highly successful financial institutions running poorly disguised PONZI schemes.

It's never about the policy. They are interested only in the amount of money they can scam, and hang on to by evasion tactics by any means, after their policyholders file claims.

This is chicanery at its worst.

That is why there are more licensed and bonded public insurance adjusters practicing in Florida today.

Someone has to provide the attorneys with the information and documentation they require to properly assist homeowners to recover the money they are entitled to under their policies, when the insurance companies do not want to pay claims as they promised to do.

Most public adjusters in practice in Florida today came from the senior ranks of insurance company claims professionals who operated by the (old) rules of professionalism, honesty and integrity.

But when Deny, Delay and Defend, the "Plague", was born they found that they could not continue to be employed by, or owe allegiance to any part of an organization that pays its employees to deliberately scam its customers, by misrepresenting policy coverages, and short-changing them on legitimate claims, which conduct they found to be not only distasteful, but also dishonest and probably fraudulent and thereby illegal and criminal.

While celebrating their growth of profits beyond their wildest dreams, insurance company CEOs, when talking to the media, whine, whinge, and bleat about the high cost of handling claims, alleging inflated invoices, escalating attorneys' fees and costs, and public adjusters inflated estimates associated with some losses caused by less attractive perils which they insure.

The unspoken truth is that the "escalation" of some legal fees and costs that are sometimes incurred necessarily to collect proper, fair and reasonable settlements that are due to insured policyholders, and are the deliberate, intentional and direct consequences of their voluntary adoption of the McKinsey claims handling doctrine and practices, and the additional legal costs associated with that conduct.

Those CEOs and Boards of Directors made a conscious decision to adopt the McKinsey doctrine of claims handling practices, but when following those guidelines and practices, complain about the costs of using that system, and the effect they have on their excessive, and ill-gotten profits when they are diluted.

However, the bare truth is that their POLICYHOLDERS have no duty or obligation, whatsoever, to "bail them out" via increased premiums, after those executive managers have made unwise, dishonest and illegal and perhaps criminal decisions, resulting in allegedly, increased operating costs leading to lower profits.

Nowhere in the insurance industry, is there a system, anywhere in the world, which guarantees a profit, at any level, for an insurance company.

Like every other business, management executives must live by their decisions. If profits decline, reduce overhead expenses, and operating costs.

The insurance industry is the only industry, certainly in the United States, where its customers are openly and flagrantly fleeced, with impunity, without any fear of accountability to official regulators, or any other meaningful consequences of any description.

If stockbrokers, for example, ignored the laws and regulations which govern their professional practices, their Regulators at the Securities and Exchange Commission would (and have, many times), taken swift action, with fines and criminal prosecutions, often resulting in prison sentences and, moreover, banishment for life from ever practicing in that profession again.

Until the recent past, the majority of policyholders who file a claim had no knowledge of the options open to them to help them obtain a fair and reasonable settlement from their insurers, by fighting for a proper and promised recovery.

They just did not realize that there were alternatives available to them to fight their insurance companies.

Florida homeowners, and not the insurance companies, are now holding the ball.

Make full use of that assistance now available.

CHAPTER 18

TEN REASONS TO CALL A PUBLIC ADJUSTER
BEFORE YOU CALL YOUR INSURANCE COMPANY

1. Your public adjuster will attend at the damaged property, before he files a claim on your behalf with the insurance company.

   If the damage to the property is of an "emergency" nature , meaning that decisions have to be made quickly and decisively, and if you have made arrangements with a public adjuster to hire him if you suffer a loss, and you have his phone number, call him and he will advise you and prevent you from making an innocent "mis-step" which might cause problems later on, an place your claim in jeopardy.

2. It is important that a public adjuster attends at the damaged property before the insurance company's field adjuster because he will then have an opportunity to discover any hidden damage which he can bring to the company's field adjuster' attention during his first visit to the property, thereby ensuring that he is aware of the hidden damage from the outset of his involvement.

3. Having inspected the damaged property, your public adjuster will file the claim with your insurance company, which also ensures that he is in control of your claim, before the company's field adjuster seeks to control the handling of your claim, which may not be in your best interests.

4. Your public adjuster will contact the company's field adjuster, and in liaison with you, will make an appointment for a joint inspection of the damaged property.

5. At that joint inspection, your public adjuster will point out to the company's field adjuster any matters which need to be brought to his attention, which need to be included in the Field adjuster's estimate.

6. You may be asked by the company's field adjuster to give a recorded statement during that first visit of the field adjuster to the damaged property.

7. FAPIA Attorneys advise against giving a recorded statement to the insurance company's field adjuster during that first visit to the damaged property. There are several reasons for the request for a recorded statement, which may be included in your policy as a "Condition" making the giving of a recorded statement mandatory. While the

giving of a recorded statement may be mandatory, that does not mean that you must give the statement when the company's adjuster requests it. Like, right then and now.

One of the reasons a recorded statement is required by the insurance company, or so they will tell you, is to determine the facts of how, when, where and when the loss occurred, if there is coverage for the cause of loss, and if so the extent of their liability.

However, there is another reason for requesting a recorded statement, which the insurance company will deny, but everyone in the claims business knows recognizes this reason.

This secondary reason is to try to entrap you into giving an answer to a question, on the spur of the moment, of the "have you stopped beating your wife?" category. Remember, in today's insurance market, the insurance company is not your friend, nor are any of their employees your friends. If they can find a way to deny your claim, they will use it, every time.

8.   Your public adjuster will protect your interests exclusively throughout the claim's process and progress, and he will ensure that the policyholder

does not unknowingly place the claim in jeopardy, either by doing, or saying, something which would be inadvisable.

9.   Your public adjuster will answer any questions you may have and will also ensure that you provide the insurers with any, and all documentation that is required to prove your claim.

10. Your public adjuster will prepare what is called a Sworn Statement in Proof of Loss, which is a document which sets out your policy obligations to give details of your claim, under oath, including the amount you are formally claiming under your policy for your loss. In essense, it is a statement of your claim.

INFORMATION FOR
POLICYHOLDER'S GUIDANCE

The policyholder needs to understand the following, which cannot be emphasized too much.

- The insurance company's field adjuster is not your friend. If he can close your claim without the company paying anything, he has done his job.

- The insurance company's desk adjuster is not your friend, for the same reason.

- Their job is to make your claim go away, and if that means being thoroughly unpleasant to you and being as difficult as possible, in the hope of getting you to accept a low-balled and short settlement, they have done their jobs.

- Remember this always. If the insurance company can close your claim file without making a payment to you their satisfaction is guaranteed.

Your public adjuster will do everything in his power to make sure you receive a settlement which is fair, reasonable and in accordance with the terms and conditions of your insurance policy, and in compliance with Florida Statute Laws, Florida Case Law, and the rules of the Department of Insurance.

CHAPTER 19

DEFENSE ATTORNEY'S COMMENTS

After the conclusion of a Deposition a couple of years ago, taken by a deservedly respected defense attorney retained by Citizens on a very small water damage loss, now in its seventh year of litigation and with the third firm of defense attorneys representing Citizens, we were talking about claims generally, and with my tongue firmly in my cheek, I stated to him that I did not understand Citizens' claims handling practices, and their general business plan.

I said to him that we always win, eventually, and probably obtain a settlement close to what was demanded initially; and yet, Citizens spends sometimes hundreds of thousands of dollars in legal fees and costs irrespective of the amount of the loss.

The attorney replied, "It is a very good business plan, because only one policyholder in seven or eight hundred claims hires a public adjuster, which leads to an attorney. The rest either settle for a small percentage of the claim, or just quite simply walk away from their claim.

The moral of the story is: "Don't let them get away with it." Fight for every dime you are entitled to, and when you have a claim, always, always hire a public adjuster.

You will not regret it.

The policyholder has nothing to lose, but time! And, he has everything to gain.

Visit our Website

www.FLHOGuide.com

CHAPTER 20
THE TEN BEST INSURANCE COMPANIES
WHEN YOU HAVE A CLAIM

1. Florida Family Insurance Company

2. St. Johns Insurance Company

3. United Services Insurance Assn. (USAA)

4. United Property & Casualty Insurance Co.

5. Tower Hill Companies

6. Cypress P & C Insurance Co.

7. Geo Vera Specialty Insurance Co.

8. AMICA Insurance

9. Anchor P & C Insurance Co.

10. Sawgrass Mutual Insurance Co.

CHAPTER 21
THE TEN WORST INSURANCE COMPANIES
WHEN YOU HAVE A CLAIM

1. People's Trust Insurance.

2. Universal P & C Insurance.

3. Heritage P & C Insurance Co.

4. Citizens Property Insurance Corp.

5. Allstate Companies.

6. Nationwide Insurance.

7. State Farm Companies.

8. Liberty Mutual Insurance Co.

9. QBE Insurance.

10 First Protective Insurance Co.

CHAPTER 22

FLORIDA HOMEOWNER'S
BILL OF RIGHTS

Florida Homeowners have the right to:

1. Receive from your insurance company an acknowledgment of your reported claim within fourteen (14) days of reporting the loss to them.

2. Upon written request, receive from your insurance company, within thirty (30) days after you have submitted a Sworn Statement in Proof of Loss to your insurance company, confirmation that your claim is covered, in full, by your policy, partially covered or denied; or receive a written statement that your claim is being investigated.

3. Within ninety (90) days, subject to any dual interest in the policy, receive full settlement payment for your claim, or the "undisputed funds" portion of your claim, or your insurance company's denial of your claim.

4. Free mediation of your disputed claim, if your claim is for damage by a sinkhole and is covered by your policy.

5.   Neutral re-evaluation of your disputed claim, if your claim for damage is caused by a sinkhole and is covered by your policy.

6.   Contact the Florida Department of Financial Services, toll free help line for assistance with any insurance claim, or questions pertaining to the handling of your claim.

You can contact the FLDFS Consumer Services Help Line by phone at **1 877 693 5236**, or you can seek assistance on line at the Department of Financial Services, Division of Consumer affairs at:

https://apps/fldfs.com/SERVICE/Default.aspx

CHAPTER 23

FLORIDA HOMEOWNERS
BILL OF RIGHTS

Florida Homeowners are advised to:

1. Contact your retained Licensed and Bonded Public Adjuster, or your insurance company, **BEFORE** entering into any contract for repairs to confirm any managed repair policy provisions, or optional and/or preferred vendors and/or contractors.

2. Make detailed notes, document and photograph all emergency repairs to prevent further damage. Keep the damaged property if feasible; keep all receipts for emergency work done.

3. Read any and every contract you are asked to sign very carefully to see if you are required to pay any out of pocket expenses, or if a fee that is based upon a percentage of the insurance proceeds that you will receive for repairing or replacing your damaged property.

4. Confirm that every contractor, or sub-contractor, you may choose to hire, is licensed in the State of Florida. You can verify any contractors' licenses and check to see if there are any complaints filed

against him, by calling the Florida Department of Business and Professional Regulation at:

1 850 487 1395.

5.   Require all Contractors, or sub-contractors to provide proof of Workers Compensation insurance, before starting any repairs.

6.   Take precautions if the damage requires you to leave your home, including securing your property, and turning off the gas, water and electricity services; and contact your insurance company and provide them with a phone number where you can be contacted.

CHAPTER 24

HURRICANE PREPAREDNESS AND CHECK LIST

Whether or not you are faced with having to evacuate from your home, it is important that you have the basics available to see you through at least seven (7) days, without power, or perhaps worse. The basics are:

- 0   None-perishable food.
- 0   Bottled water - (three cases per person)
- 0   First aid supplies, including all medications
- 0   Persona hygiene and sanitation supplies
- 0   Flashlights & extra batteries
- 0   Waterproof container for cash and important papers and documents
- 0   Manual can opener
- 0   Lighter (and fuel therefor) or matches
- 0   Propane stove and cans of propane gas
- 0   Books, magazines and games
- 0   Baby and pet supplies, food and medications
- 0   Cooler for ice
- 0   A plan for emergency evacuation
- 0   Location of nearest emergency shelter for family and pets.
- 0   Location of place where family can meet if they become separated
- 0   Cell phone, and charging cables
- 0   Portable battery/hand generated radio with USB charging cable outlets.

CHAPTER 25

ATLANTIC HURRICANE NAMES - 2018

No	NAME	DATE(S)	CAT	REMARKS
1	ALBERTO			
2	BERYL			
3	CHRIS			
4	DEBBY			
5	ERNESTO			
6	GORDON			
7	HELENE			
8	ISAAC			
9	JOYCE			
10	KIRK			
11	LESLIE			
12	MICHAEL			
13	NADINE			

14	OSCAR			
15	PATTY			
16	RAPHAEL			
17	SARA			
18	TROY			
19	VALERIE			
20	WILLIAM			
21				
22				
23				
24				
25				
26				
27				

CHAPTER 26

UNDISPUTED FUNDS

When you file a property claim on your insured dwelling, and during the process and progress of your claim through the system, your insurance company may send you a check, perhaps with an estimate attached, for the amount of their estimate and an offer to settle your claim for the amount of their check, net of your deductible and, under certain circumstances, a deduction for depreciation. The amount of their offer will be the amount shown on the face of their check, which should match the estimate.

You may believe that the amount offered is insufficient to enable you to make repairs and restore the property to its pre-loss condition. You are probably right!

In this situation you may be unsure of your position. What do you do with the check, if you wish to pursue your claim for more money.

The amount shown on the face of the check, for which amount the insurance company is offering to settle your claim is called "undisputed funds".

In short, you may cash this check, or deposit it in your bank account without prejudicing your right to pursue your claim for more money. Your public adjuster will write to your insurance company advising them that you are accepting their check, as "undisputed funds" only, and that you propose to pursue your claim for a full indemnity for your loss.

In general terms, it is true that if you receive a check for example, a "slip and fall" claim, and you cash or bank the check, this is regarded as an acceptance of their offer to settle, and the amount paid to you and cashed or banked is a "confession of judgement," and your claim file will be closed.

However, in Florida, on a first party homeowners property claim the acceptance of "undisputed funds" does not close your claim, and you may proceed in any way you see fit to obtain a full indemnity for your loss, and you receive a fair and reasonable settlement as promised by your insurance policy.

Warning: There are some insurance companies, including Universal Property and Casualty Insurance Company of Fort Lauderdale, Florida that have started to issue "offer of settlement" checks or drafts, which include language on the back of the check/draft, where you would endorse it to deposit it in your bank, which purports to be a "Full Release and Discharge " of your claim.

This is a typical "Universal" ploy to try to trick you into accepting a low-balled offer to settle your claim.

Since the inception of Universal into the Florida insurance marketplace in the late 1990s, Universal has issued "drafts," instead of checks, which have to be sent to Universal for verification and approval before you receive "value" for your draft deposit in your bank account. The reason for this is that Universal has an additional week or ten days before those funds are debited to their bank account, and the daily interest adds up.

Other insurance companies may try to pull the same scam (Full Release and Discharge language on the back of a check in offer of settlement) to try to trick you into accepting a low-balled settlement. However, the consensus of opinion among FAPIA attorneys is that this underhand trickery to try and convert a payment for "undisputed funds" into a final settlement, will not prevail in a Florida Court. If you receive such a check, you would be well advised to check with an attorney who is familiar with Florida, first party property claims, to clarify your position, before you bank the check or draft.

Usually, these "undisputed funds" checks, or drafts, are about 20% of the actual amount you are entitled to recover under your policy.

It's that PONZI scheme working again!

CHAPTER 27

UNIVERSAL PROPERTY AND CASUALTY
INSURANCE COMPANY

Instant or Immediate Settlements

Reportedly, Universal Property and Casualty Insurance Company is currently test running a claims handling program called an "Instant or Immediate Settlement" Program, for which Florida homeowners need to be prepared, and this program should be viewed with great suspicion.

This scheme or program is different to the 'Undisputed Funds" issue discussed in the previous chapter.

It has been reported that Universal has given certain field adjusters the authority to offer some policyholders an "instant" or "immediate" settlement of their claim. This occurs at the conclusion of the field adjuster's first attendance on site, after he has written and priced a "scope of loss" and has written an "estimate" of the repair costs. Obviously, to make this program work, Universal has provided a select few field adjusters to test the program and a supply of blank drafts to issue in settlement on the claim.

But, there is a serious snag to this pilot program.

In exchange for issuing a draft to the policyholder supposedly in settlement of the claim, the policyholder is required to sign a **FULL RELEASE AND DISCHARGE** of the claim, in favor of Universal, and this would effectively end the policyholder's claim and the claim file would be closed.

The **"Instant"** and **"Immediate"** settlement program should raise a very large red flag.

Universal's policyholders should be aware that ever since Universal first opened its doors for business, policyholders have experienced, first hand, their unfair and illegal claims handling practices, which include a general policy of writing low-balled estimates and unethical and illegal claims handling practices, and very short settlements.

Universal's policyholders who file a claim, and then are offered an "Instant" and/or "Immediate" settlement should be extremely cautious, and they would be well advised to consult a public adjuster, and seek his opinion as to whether the amount being offered in settlement is fair and reasonable.

CHAPTER 28

FLORIDA STATUTES RELATING TO THE ADJUSTMENT OF FIRST PARTY PROPERTY CLAIMS FLORIDA 2018/19

Fs. 626.8548 - "All Lines Adjuster:"

An "All Lines" Adjuster is a person who is self-employed, or employed by an insurer, a wholly owned subsidiary of an insurer, or an independent adjusting form or another independent adjuster who undertakes on behalf of an insurer, or other insurers under common control or ownership to ascertain and determine the amount of any claim, loss or damage, payable under an insurance contract, or undertakes to effect settlement of such claim, loss or damage.

Fs. 626.855 - "Independent Adjuster:"

An "Independent Adjuster" mean a person licensed as an "All Lines" adjuster who is self-employed, or appointed or employed by an independent adjusting firm, or other independent adjuster, and who undertakes on behalf of the insurer to ascertain and determine the amount of any claim, loss or damage, payable under an insurance contract, or undertakes to effect settlement of such claim, loss or damage.

NOTE: *This definition is misleading and it will be noted that, by Florida statutory definition, an "independent" adjuster adjusts claims only for insurers, or entities employed by insurers.*

Thus, an "Independent Adjuster" in Florida, is NOT independent in the normally accepted meaning of the term, as defined in a dictionary.

626.856 - "Company Employee Adjuster" defined:

A "Company Employee Adjuster" means a person licensed as an "All Lines" adjuster who is appointed by and employed by, or on an insurer's staff of adjusters, or a wholly owned subsidiary of the insurer, who undertakes on behalf of such insurer or other insurers under common control or ownership to ascertain and determine th amount of any claim, loss or damage, payable under a contract of insurance or undertakes to effect settlement of such claim, loss and damage.

Fs. 626.863 - Claim referrals to independent adjusters:

An insurer may not knowingly refer any claim for loss for adjustment in this state to any person purporting to be or acting as an independent adjuster unless the person is currently licensed as an "All Lines" adjuster and appointed as an independent adjuster under this code.

Fs. 626.866 - "All Lines" Adjuster qualifications:

The Department shall issue an adjuster license to an applicant upon determining that the applicable fee specified in Fs. 624.501 has been paid, and the applicant possesses the following qualifications:

Has had sufficient experience, training or instruction concerning the adjustment of damage under insurance contracts, other life or annuity contracts, and possesses adequate knowledge of the insurance laws of this state relating to such contracts as to enable him to engage in the business of adjuster fairly and without injury to the public or any member thereof with whom he or she might have relations as an insurance adjuster, and to adjust all claims in accordance with the policy or contract, and the insurance laws of this state.

Fs. 626.877 - Adjustments to comply with insurance contracts and the law:

Every adjuster shall adjust and investigate every claim, damage or loss made or occurring under an insurance contract, in accordance with the terms and condition of the policy, and the applicable laws of this state.

Fs. 626.878 - Code of Ethics:

An adjuster shall subscribe to the Code of Ethics specified by the rules of the Department. The rules shall implement the provisions of this part, and specify the terms and conditions of contracts, including the right to cancel and require practices necessary to ensure fair dealing, prohibit conflicts of interest, and ensure preservation of the rights of the claimant to participate in the adjustment of a claim.

Fs. 626.8795 - Public Adjuster; Prohibition of Conflicts of Interest:

A public adjuster shall not participate, directly or indirectly, in the reconstruction, repair or restoration of damaged property that is the subject of a claim adjusted by the licensee; may not engage in any other activities that may be construed as a conflict of interest, including the soliciting or accepting any remuneration from any person, of any kind or nature, directly or indirectly; and may not have a financial interest in any salvage, repair, or any other business entity that obtains business in connection with any claim the adjuster has a contract or an agreement to adjust.

Fs. 626-9744 (The Matching Statute)
Claim settlement practices relating to property insurance.

Unless otherwise provided by the policy, when a homeowner's insurance policy provides for the adjustment and settlement of first party losses based on repair or replacement cost, the following requirements shall apply:

(1)   When a loss requires repair of replacement of an item or part, any physical damage incurred in making such repair or replacement which is covered and not excluded by the policy shall be included in the loss to the extent of any applicable limits. The insured may not be required to pay for betterment required by ordinance or code except for the applicable Deductible.

(2)   When a loss requires repair or replacement of items and the replaced items do not match in

quality, color or size, the insurer shall make reasonable repairs or replacements in adjoining areas. In determining the extent of repair or replacement of items in adjoining areas, the insurer may consider the cost of repairing or replacing the undamaged portions of the property, the degree of uniformity that can be achieved without such cost, the remaining useful life of the undamaged portion, and other relevant factors.

(3)   This section shall not make the insurer a warrantor of the repairs made pursuant to this section.

(4)   Nothing in this section shall be construed to authorize or preclude enforcement of policy provisions relating to settlement disputes.

NB. Florida case law: This statute includes, "Line of sight."

CHAPTER 29

A FINAL WORD

A wise and prudent homeowner must think twice, three times or maybe, even five times, before entrusting the handling of his claim to his insurance company, whose employees are trained with the express intention of low-balling and under paying your claim, sometimes to fraudulent levels.

It has to be borne in mind that insurance companies have a long and proven history, now going back twenty-five (25) years, of knowingly and deliberately underpaying claims settlements to its policyholders, as a daily common practice. They believe your proper claims proceeds are better left in their bank account, instead of remitting those proceeds to the policyholder, as promised by their policies.

Today's Vice Presidents of claims, and most claims managers have spent their entire careers systematically underpaying their policyholders, with impunity, and thumbing their noses at not only their policyholders, but at official, government regulators, whose job it is to protect insured consumers against predatory operators of poorly disguised PONZI schemes, posing as insurance companies.

A very prudent homeowner/policyholder who is unfortunate enough to suffer a covered loss and file a claim against his insurance company, should consult a policyholder's claims expert, a licensed and bonded public adjuster before he talks to anyone else. The average public adjuster has much more knowledge about claims, claims law, and the proper handling of insurance claims that any field adjuster currently working for an insurance company.

Company employee adjusters, by the thousands, are inadequately trained to scope a loss, are totally ignorant of the Florida statutes which govern how claims are to be investigated and adjusted, whose only purpose is to close your claim for the absolute lowest sum you are willing to accept, and he is backed up by insurance company executives who have no ethics, and no integrity whatsoever. If they can cheat you into believing you do not have a valid claim, and get away with it, they have done their job.

Those are the facts.

The profession of public adjusting has grown exponentially since Hurricane "Andrew" which devastated Florida in 1991. At that time, there were less than 300 licensed public adjusters in Florida. Today, with the introduction to the marketplace of the McKinsey doctrine of Deny, Delay and Defend as the preferred tool for handling claims, with a goal of defrauding Florida homeowners out of their proper indemnity, there are now close to 2,000 licensed public adjusters in Florida, down from a high of almost 3,000 after Hurricane "Wilma."

These dedicated, knowledgeable and experienced professional public adjusters are fighting, every day, for proper, fair and reasonable settlements for their clients.

The premier licensed and bonded public adjusters practicing in Florida are members of the Florida Association of Public Insurance Adjusters, FAPIA.

To learn more about FAPIA visit their website at: www. FAPIA.net.

You will be in safe hands, and you will receive the benefit of unequaled, professional handling of your claim.

You will not be sorry.

Martyn G. D. Belben
Fort Lauderdale, Florida
March, 2018

POST SCRIPT

PLAINTIFF'S ATTORNEYS ADVERTISING
ON TELEVISION AND RADIO IN SOUTH FLORIDA

There is a firm of Plaintiff's attorneys advertising their services on Television and Radio in South Florida, stating or implying that they have been very successful in handling plumbing and/or water damage claims against insurance companies, and have had success in getting insurance companies to "re-pipe" plumbing installations, including underground supply and drain pipes. The television "clips" show cracked, broken and leaking cast iron pipes, which appear to have lived their useful life and need replacement because of "wear and tear," and "gradual deterioration," which are excluded perils, or causes of loss in every property insurance policy in the world.

In my almost sixty five (65) years of handling civil engineering, property and marine insurance claims, worldwide, I have never seen nor heard of any insurance company, anywhere, that has paid to "re-pipe" a plumbing system, where pipes apparently, have been damaged by wear and tear and/or gradual deterioration.

Insurance policies are not maintenance contracts. They do not cover something that is going to happen, sooner or later. They cover events that MIGHT happen, under certain circumstances. There is an exception, of course, for life insurance policies, which were and are created for a different purpose.

There is one exception to my re-piping comments.

About twenty five (25) years ago, maybe longer, a large, multi -national oil company invented a material which it intended to be used in residential plumbing systems. The material was cheaper than copper pipes and fittings, and easier to install during the construction process.

The material was a plastic type material, called Polybutylene, and extruded pipes, and molded fittings were manufactured and installed in thousands of homes. The fittings were "finger tight" and after two or three years these systems failed.

Of course, the oil company was sued, and a class action award was made to allow for the complete replacement of these plumbing systems, usually with PVC materials, which was paid for by the oil company, who set up a trust fund to meet the costs.

Caveat Emptor! Do your homework.

CHAPTER 30

TOP TWENTY-FIVE FLORIDA

HOMEOWNERS INSURANCE COMPANIES

BY NUMBER OF POLICIES IN FORCE AS AT

December, 2017

01	UNIVERSAL PROPERTY & CASUALTY INS. CO.	
Address	1110 West Commercial Boulevard, Ste, 300	
	Fort Lauderdale, Florida 33309	
Phones	954 958 1200	
Email	universalproperty.com	
CEO	SEAN P. DOWNES	
As at December, 2017		
Policies in Force		577,263
UNDERWRITING ACCOUNT, 2016		
Underwriting Revenue/Premium		$853,994,909
Claim Paid		$214,496,774
Net Revenue		$639,498135
PREMIUM INCREASES APPROVED		
2016		10.00%
2018		9.90%

NOTES

02	CITIZENS PROPERTY INSURANCE CORP.	
Address	2312 Killearn Center Boulevard	
	Tallahassee, Florida 32309	
Phones	850 513 3700	
Email	citizensfla.com	
CEO	**Barry Gilway**	
AS OF DECEMBER, 2017		
Policies in Force		466,506
UNDERWRITING ACCOUNT - 2016		
Underwriting Revenue/Premium		$973,840,305
Claims Paid		$344,926,118
Net Premium/Revenue		$628,914,187
PREMIUM INCREASES APPROVED		
Varies by Location - Check for 2018		

NOTES

03	SECURITY FIRST INSURANCE COMPANY	
Address	140 South Atlantic Boulevard	
	Ormond Beach, Florida 32176	
Phones	386 673 5308	
email	securityfirstflorida.com	
CEO	W. Lockwood Burt	
AS OF DECEMBER, 2017		
Policies in Force		334,335
UNDERWRITING ACCOUNT - 2016		
Underwriting Revenue/Premium		$360,519,222
Claims Paid		$209,453,341
Net Premium/Revenue		$151,065,881
PREMIUM INCREASES APPROVED		
Unavailable going to press		

NOTES

04	FEDERATED NATIONAL (FEDNAT) INS. CO.	
Address	14040 N. W. 14th. Street	
	Sunrise, Florida 33323	
Phones	954 581 9993	
email	fednat.com	
CEO	**Michael Braun**	
AS OF DECEMBER, 2017		
Policies in Force		272,335
UNDERWRITING ACCOUNT - 2016		
Underwriting Revenue/Premium		$497,085,385
Claims Paid		$210,140,464
Net Premium/Revenue		$286,944,921
PREMIUM INCREASES APPROVED		
Unavailable going to press		

NOTES

05	HERITAGE PROPERTY & CASUALTY INS. CO..
Address	700 Central Avenue
	St. Petersburg, Florida 33701
Phones	727 362 7200
email	heritagepci.com
CEO	Richard Widdecombe
AS OF DECEMBER, 2017	
Policies in Force	241,822
UNDERWRITING ACCOUNT - 2016	
Underwriting Revenue/Premium	$570,078,756
Claims Paid	$179,570,756
Net Premium/Revenue	$390,507,386
PREMIUM INCREASES APPROVED	
Reportedly requested -	10.0%
Be advised: Be aware: "Right to Repair Clause."	

NOTES

06	AMERICAN INTEGRITY INS. CO. OF FLORIDA	
Address	7650 West Courtney Campbell Park, Ste 12	
	Tampa, Florida 33607	
Phones	850 513 3700	
email	aiicfl.com	
CEO	**Robert Ritchie**	
AS OF DECEMBER, 2017		
Policies in Force		236,796
UNDERWRITING ACCOUNT - 2016		
Underwriting Revenue/Premium		$262,360,433
Claims Paid		$84,076,709
Net Premium/Revenue		$178,283,724
PREMIUM INCREASES APPROVED		
Unavailable going to press.		

NOTES

07	UNITED PROPERTY & CASUALTY INS. CO.	
Address	P.O. Box 1011,	
	St. Petersburg, Florida 33731	
Phones	850 222 6656	
email	upcinsurance.com	
CEO	John Fortney	
AS OF DECEMBER, 2017		
Policies in Force		187,412
UNDERWRITING ACCOUNT - 2016		
Underwriting Revenue/Premium		$341,371,560
Claims Paid		$142,210,617
Net Premium/Revenue		$199,160,943
PREMIUM INCREASES APPROVED		
Unavailable going to press.		

NOTES

08	St. JOHNS INSURANCE COMPANY.	
Address	6675 Westwood Boulevard, Ste. 360,	
	Orlando, Florida 32821	
Phones	407 226 8460	
email	stjohnsinsurance.com	
CEO	**Reece Brown**	
AS OF DECEMBER, 2017		
Policies in Force		166,396
UNDERWRITING ACCOUNT - 2016		
Underwriting Revenue/Premium		$249,457,778
Claims Paid		$120,787,727
Net Premium/Revenue		$128,670,051
PREMIUM INCREASES APPROVED		
Unavailable going to press		

NOTES

09	HOMEOWNERS CHOICE P & C INS. CO.	
Address	5300 West Cypress Street, Ste 100,	
	Tampa, Florida 33607	
Phones	727 213 3600	
email	hcpci.com	
CEO	**Parash Patel**	
AS OF DECEMBER, 2017		
Policies in Force		149,793
UNDERWRITING ACCOUNT - 2016		
Underwriting Revenue/Premium		$Unavailable
Claims Paid		$Unavailable
Net Premium/Revenue		$Unavailable
PREMIUM INCREASES APPROVED		
Unavailable going to press.		

NOTES

10	TOWER HILL PRIME INSURANCE COMPANY.	
Address	P. O. Box 147018,	
	Gainesville, Florida 32614	
Phones	850 894 2777	
email	thig.com	
CEO	**Paresh Patel**	
AS OF DECEMBER, 2017		
Policies in Force		148,377
UNDERWRITING ACCOUNT - 2016		
Underwriting Revenue/Premium		$281,368.393
Claims Paid		$118,945,452
Net Premium/Revenue		$162,422,941
PREMIUM INCREASES APPROVED		
Varies by Location - Check for 2018		

NOTES

11	PEOPLES TRUST INSURANCE CO.	
Address	18 People's Trust Way,	
	Deerfield Beach, Florida 33441	
Phones	508 915 4829	
email	ptiinsure.com	
CEO	George Schaeffer	
AS OF DECEMBER, 2017		
Policies in Force		146,106
UNDERWRITING ACCOUNT - 2016		
Underwriting Revenue/Premium		$266,552,943
Claims Paid		$158,184,701
Net Premium/Revenue		$108,368,242
PREMIUM INCREASES APPROVED		
Varies by Location - Check for 2018		
Be Advised. Be Aware "Right to Repair Clause"		

NOTES

12	ASI PREFERRED INSURANCE COMPANY	
Address	P.O. Box 33018	
	St. Petersburg, Florida 33733	
Phones	727 821 8765	
email	americanstrategic.com	
CEO	John Auer	
AS OF DECEMBER, 2017		
Policies in Force		125,537
UNDERWRITING ACCOUNT - 2016		
Underwriting Revenue/Premium		$145,534,211
Claims Paid		$39,754,524
Net Premium/Revenue		$105,779,687
PREMIUM INCREASES APPROVED		
Unavailable going to press.		

NOTE

13	UNITED SERVICES AUTO ASSN. (USAA)	
Address	17200 Commerce Park Boulevard,	
	Tampa, Florida 33647	
Phones	813 615 5222	
email	usaa.com	
CEO	Stuart Parker	
AS OF DECEMBER, 2017		
Policies in Force		124,157
UNDERWRITING ACCOUNT - 2016		
Underwriting Revenue/Premium (Corporate)		$736,838,512
Claims Paid (Corporate)		$458,928,965
Net Premium/Revenue (Corporate)		$522,341,738
PREMIUM INCREASES APPROVED		
Unavailable going to press.		

NOTES

14	FLORIDA PENINSULA INSURANCE COMPANY	
Address	903 N.W. 56th. Street,	
	Boca Raton, Florida 33487	
Phones	561 994 8366	
email	floridapeninsula.com	
CEO	Clint Strauch	
AS OF DECEMBER, 2017		
Policies in Force		118,771
UNDERWRITING ACCOUNT - 2016		
Underwriting Revenue/Premium		$253,937,771
Claims Paid		$89,339,628
Net Premium/Revenue		$164,598,143
PREMIUM INCREASES APPROVED		
Unavailable going to press.		

NOTES

15	FIRST PROTECTIVE INSURANCE COMPANY	
Address	7131 Business Park Lane,	
	Lake Mary, Florida 32746	
Phones	407 444 5224	
email	frontlineinsurance.com	
CEO	**Lemon Porter**	
AS OF DECEMBER, 2017		
Policies in Force		104,138
UNDERWRITING ACCOUNT - 2016		
Underwriting Revenue/Premium		$265,922,707
Claims Paid		$107,887,640
Net Premium/Revenue		$158,035,067
PREMIUM INCREASES APPROVED		
Unavailable going to press.		

NOTES

16	CASTLE KEY INDEMNITY CO. (ALLSTATE)	
Address	780 Carillon Parkway	
	St. Petersburg, Florida 33716	
Phones	727 777 6862	
email	allstate.com	
CEO	**Mike Sheely (Florida)**	
AS OF DECEMBER, 2017		
Policies in Force		99,943
UNDERWRITING ACCOUNT - 2016		
Underwriting Revenue/Premium		$103,538,652
Claims Paid		$49,032,150
Net Premium/Revenue		$54,506,502
PREMIUM INCREASES APPROVED		
Unavailable going to press.		

NOTES

17	FLORIDA FAMILY INSURANCE COMPANY	
Address	P. O Box 136001	
	Bonita Springs, Florida 34136	
Phones	888 850 4663	
email	floridafamily.com	
CEO	John Fortney	
AS OF DECEMBER, 2017		
Policies in Force		98,089
UNDERWRITING ACCOUNT - 2016		
Underwriting Revenue/Premium		$113,195,609
Claims Paid		$63,333,451
Net Premium/Revenue		$49,862,158
PREMIUM INCREASES APPROVED		
Unavailable going to press.		
NB. No wind Coverage. (Wind Policy (Citizens))		

NOTES

18	AMERICAN BANKERS INS. CO. (ASSURANT)	
Address	11222 Quail Roost Drive,	
	Miami, Florida 33157	
Phones	305 253 2244 - 1 800 852 2244	
email	assurantsolutions.com	
CEO	**Patricia Mulvania (Florida)**	
AS OF DECEMBER, 2017		
Policies in Force		94,374
UNDERWRITING ACCOUNT - 2016		
Underwriting Revenue/Premium		$Unavailable
Claims Paid		$Unavailable
Net Premium/Revenue		$Unavailable
PREMIUM INCREASES APPROVED		
Unavailable going to press		
Forced Place coverage specialist		

NOTES

19	ARK ROYAL INSURANCE COMPANY (ASI Group)	
Address	805 Executive Center Drive, Ste 300	
	St. Petersburg, Florida 33702	
Phones	727 456 1673	
email	americanstrategic.com	
CEO	John Auer	
AS OF DECEMBER, 2017		
Policies in Force		94,374
UNDERWRITING ACCOUNT - 2016		
Underwriting Revenue/Premium		$Unavailable
Claims Paid		$Unavailable
Net Premium/Revenue		$Unavailable
PREMIUM INCREASES APPROVED		
Unavailable going to press		

NOTES

20	TOWER HILL SIGNATURE INSURANCE CO.	
Address	P.O. Box 14718,	
	Gainesville, Florida 33614	
Phones	800 509 1592	
email	thig.com	
CEO	**Donald Matz**	
AS OF DECEMBER, 2017		
Policies in Force		85257
UNDERWRITING ACCOUNT - 2016		
Underwriting Revenue/Premium		$135,487,083
Claims Paid		$56,751,052
Net Premium/Revenue		$78,736,031
PREMIUM INCREASES APPROVED		
Unavailable going to press.		

NOTES

21	OLYMPUS INSURANCE COMPANY	
Address	7380 West Sand Lake Road, Ste. 115	
	Orlando, Florida 32818	
Phones	321 558 3954	
email	olympusinsurance.com	
CEO	Jeffrey Scott	
AS OF DECEMBER, 2017		
Policies in Force		82,320
UNDERWRITING ACCOUNT - 2016		
Underwriting Revenue/Premium		$132,365,611
Claims Paid		$56,708,589
Net Premium/Revenue		$75,657,022
PREMIUM INCREASES APPROVED		
Unavailable going to press.		

NOTES

22	SAFE HARBOR INSURANCE COMPANY.	
Address	2549 Barrington Circle	
	Tallahassee, Florida 32308	
Phones	321 558 3954	
email	claims@harborclaims.com	
CEO	Unavailable	
AS OF DECEMBER, 2017		
Policies in Force		78337
UNDERWRITING ACCOUNT - 2016		
Underwriting Revenue/Premium		$Unavailable
Claims Paid		$Unavailable
Net Premium/Revenue		$Unavailable
PREMIUM INCREASES APPROVED		
Unavailable going to press.		

NOTES

23	CASTLE KEY INSURANCE COMPANY (ALLSTATE)	
Address	780 Carillon Parkway	
	St. Petersburg, Florida 33716	
Phones	727 777 6862	
email	allstate.com	
CEO	Michael Sheely (Florida)	
AS OF DECEMBER, 2017		
Policies in Force		73,011
UNDERWRITING ACCOUNT - 2016		
Underwriting Revenue/Premium		$103,538,652
Claims Paid		$49,032,150
Net Premium/Revenue		$54,506,502
PREMIUM INCREASES APPROVED		
Unavailable going to press.		

NOTES

24	SAFEPOINT INSURANCE COMPANY	
Address	8761 North 56th Street	
	Temple Terrace, Florida 33617	
Phones	877 858 7445	
email	safepointins.com	
CEO	**Nancy Bailey - Claims VP. Rodney Ward**	
AS OF DECEMBER, 2017		
Policies in Force		70,675
UNDERWRITING ACCOUNT - 2016		
Underwriting Revenue/Premium		$Unavailable
Claims Paid		$Unavailable
Net Premium/Revenue		$Unavailable
PREMIUM INCREASES APPROVED		
Unavailable going to press.		

NOTES

25	CYPRESS PROPERTY & CASUALTY INS. CO.	
Address	12926 Gran Bay Parkway West, Ste. 200,	
	Jacksonville, Florida 32258	
Phones	1800 560 5224 - 904 438 3866	
email	cypressig.com	
CEO	**Edna McDonell**	
AS OF DECEMBER, 2017		
Policies in Force		68,723
UNDERWRITING ACCOUNT - 2016		
Underwriting Revenue/Premium		$Unavailable
Claims Paid		$Unavailable
Net Premium/Revenue		$Unavailable
PREMIUM INCREASES APPROVED		
Unavailable going to press.		

NOTES

NOTES

NOTES

www.ingramcontent.com/pod-product-compliance
Lightning Source LLC
Chambersburg PA
CBHW070630240526
45467CB00050B/97